− Outplacement and Inplacement Counseling −

LAWRENCE M. BRAMMER
University of Washington

FRANK E. HUMBERGER
Executive Services Associates

PRENTICE-HALL, INC., Englewood Cliffs, New Jersey 07632

658.3
B 81

Library of Congress Cataloging in Publication Data

Brammer, Lawrence M.
  Outplacement and inplacement counseling.

  Includes bibliographical references and index.
  1. Employee counseling.   2. Employees, Dismissal of.
3. Executives—Dismissal of.   4. Career changes.   5. Job
hunting.   I. Humberger, Frank E.   II. Title.
HF5549.5.C8B7   1984   658.3'85   83-21263
ISBN 0-13-645227-2

Editorial/production supervision and interior design: Barbara Grasso
Cover design: Lundgren Graphics, Ltd.
Manufacturing buyer: Ed O'Dougherty

This book is available to businesses and organizations at a special discount when ordered in large quantities. For information, contact Prentice-Hall, Inc., General Book Marketing, Special Sales Division, Englewood Cliffs, N.J. 07632.

Printed in the United States of America

10   9   8   7   6   5   4   3   2   1

ISBN 0-13-645227-2

Prentice-Hall International, Inc., *London*
Prentice-Hall of Australia Pty. Limited, *Sydney*
Editora Prentice-Hall do Brasil, Ltda., *Rio de Janeiro*
Prentice-Hall Canada Inc., *Toronto*
Prentice-Hall of India Private Limited, *New Delhi*
Prentice-Hall of Japan, Inc., *Tokyo*
Prentice-Hall of Southeast Asia Pte. Ltd., *Singapore*
Whitehall Books Limited, *Wellington, New Zealand*

Contents

Introduction

WHAT IS OUTPLACEMENT
AND INPLACEMENT COUNSELING?

Outplacement counseling is a process of helping terminated employees face the crisis of job loss with renewed self-esteem and to conduct a positive job placement or retraining campaign. This process is one of management's newest human resource tools. We estimate that during the past twelve years, more than 100,000 American executives and managers have been counseled by more than 300 outplacement counselors. Furthermore, several major corporations have instituted internal outplacement counseling for thousands of nonexempt hourly employees. We predict that this growth will continue, as the beneficial results of outplacement counseling services become better known.

We view outplacement counseling as part of human resource management. In this context, the interests of the employee and the corporation converge. In one sense the necessity for outplacement, apart from economic reasons, is an admission of individual or corporate failure. Therefore, if human resource management services were functioning optimally, there would be less need to terminate employees. Presently, we estimate that half of terminations for cause are employee personal failures to produce, get along, or grow. Some terminations we judge to be organizational failures to select, train, counsel, or evaluate the employees slated for termination. On the other hand, we recognize that no matter how well developed the organization's human resource programs may be, there will be occasional terminations growing out of sudden mergers, and misfits created by internal changes. We estimate that most of the remaining half of terminations are due to economic cutbacks.

1

We have chosen to call this look at alternatives to outplacement an inplacement counseling approach. In this book the authors show how this same counseling process can be used for inplacement counseling to reduce termination costs. Inplacement counseling is to the white-collar worker what retraining is to the blue-collar worker. These alternatives are explored in detail in Chapter 7, and they include career planning, early and phased retirement, employee assistance counseling, training programs, and management counseling. Just as people begin dying from the day they are born, so the new employee from the selection interview onward is preparing for termination. Outplacement counseling or inplacement counseling are culminations of this living-training-separating process. If this philosophy of optimum personnel management is applied, outplacement counseling may become less necessary in future decades.

WHAT ARE THE CANDIDATE'S GOALS IN OUTPLACEMENT COUNSELING?

The major thrust of outplacement counseling is reemployment; but the unique aspect of this book is that outplacement work goes far beyond placement in or retraining for a new job. Effective counseling focuses on rebuilding candidates' self-esteem, gaining new meaning for their lives, and finding the optimal balance of work life and family life. Thus, outplacement counselors are concerned about the total person. (In this book we refer to the person being helped as the candidate.) These tasks require a counselor who is not only an expert on careers, but is also a coach on writing résumés, an adviser on job searches, and a trainer for interviews. This effective counselor also enables candidates to perceive themselves as winners, as capable persons, and as important human beings.

The effective counselor offers assistance with a process through which candidates can discover new meanings for their lives. They become acquainted with who they really are—their wants, needs, values, hopes, loves, and pains. They explore also who they would like to be—not just in reference to a job, but also to their total lives. They come to grips with their struggles over intimacy in a time of alienation, their fears for survival in a nuclear age, and their security in recessionary times. Many candidates for outplacement counseling remember the depression of the 1930s, the war days of the 40s, the expansive 50s, the turbulent 60s, and the causes of the 70s. Candidates carry these memories, but they also are reminded daily that the 1980s have their unique challenges and threats to survival. This is the context for job campaigns and retraining of the 1980s.

Outplacement counselors and services *are not* to be confused with career consultants or counselors who charge individuals fees for occupational assessment and planning their job campaigns. Outplacement counselors do not function as search firms or employment experts. Neither are they management recruiters. Outplacement counselors are employed by organizations to assist candidates with job relocation or retraining. This service may be provided by an external firm or a human resources specialist for inplacement counseling.

WHO SHOULD READ THIS BOOK?

This book is written for managers of organizations faced with the need for increasing productivity, handling problem subordinates, or reducing staff. It is written also for executives who must decide on an out-, down-, or lateral-placement strategy, and for all helping professionals who work with employees. It is expected that this book will help readers to implement human resource management decisions that will improve one facet of productivity in their organizations. Everybody wins in outplacement counseling: the organization gets rid of troublesome situations; office morale improves; and terminated employees usually get better jobs than they had before.

This book is written especially for personnel managers, human resource specialists, and training directors charged with advising top management on the most appropriate strategy to use in termination. The first chapters will help managers to decide whether to seek the assistance of external consultants with outplacement counseling, or to do it themselves. For managers choosing the latter option, this book can serve as a map for their self-help strategy. For those choosing an external consultant, this book will help responsible managers to understand the outplacement counseling process more clearly and to choose their external consultants wisely.

Readers, in their contacts with colleagues who are being terminated, may use the principles of this book to advise those colleagues on job campaign procedures and strategies, whether in outplacement or inplacement counseling.

The terms *organization* and *corporation* are used interchangeably in the text. Governmental agencies are public corporations in a legal sense and are included when the term *corporation* is cited.

Each chapter has notes at the end referring to research cited in the text, further explanations, and suggestions for further reading. Numbers in the text are keyed to the notes. It is our intent to give credit to researchers and writers for their ideas and findings whenever possible. We are grateful to our colleagues who have contributed to the development of this field. We are especially appreciative of the helpful contributions from our colleagues of Executive Services Associates, Bellevue, Washington.

1

What Is Outplacement Counseling?

Terminating employees is a stressful task for managers and executive officers. It is difficult to inflict the pain and hardship of termination on fellow employees. Yet, organizations are concerned about increasing productivity. Outplacement counseling is a management tool for improving organizational effectiveness with a minimum of stress to executives and employees.

Goals for increasing productivity can often be met by terminating employees who are chronically unproductive, mismatched to their jobs, or in positions that are superfluous. Outplacement counseling assists those employees who are terminated to find other jobs or careers and helps them through the crisis of job loss and the pain of finding another by building renewed self-esteem and confidence. Maintaining or rebuilding the candidate's self-esteem (for our purposes, defined as the extent to which candidates believe themselves to be capable, important, worthy, and successful persons) is the most important task of the early counseling process.

Outplacement counseling services are expanding rapidly. While formerly limited to top executives, they are being offered by external consultants to all levels of management and technical staff. *The Wall Street Journal* estimates that approximately 15,000 United States executives and managers received outplacement counseling in 1981.[1] We estimate this number to be doubled in 1982. The potential for outplacement counseling of managers is enormous considering that 20 percent are unemployed at some point in their management careers.[2]

In-house outplacement counseling services are being offered to terminated hourly workers in many companies on a limited basis. Since these services are being expanded to include employees at all levels, organizations need to know how to perform this important benefit for themselves. The purpose of this book is to give managerial personnel responsible for outplacement, lateral placement, and down placement some tools and strategies to provide these outplacement counseling services. (The term *outplacement* is somewhat misleading since it does not mean placement on a new job by the counselor, but rather enables people to conduct their own job campaigns or retraining plans that lead to new jobs.) Before we discuss the counseling process in detail, we will present here a few brief examples of programs.

The Weyerhaueser forest products firm maintains a resource center that provides outplacement counseling and a current information system for all terminated professional and management employees except top executives. Candidates can maintain an office from which to conduct their job campaigns. Outside consultants are utilized for technical advice in the outplacement process and to provide the outplacement services for top-level executives.

An example in government is the outplacement program of the Goddard Flight Center. In this voluntary program, released employees are assisted in groups, supplemented by individual counseling by center personnel staff. Volunteer peer support groups are encouraged. This highly rated personnel program was evaluated by Leibowitz and Schlossberg[3] as an exemplary project.

The Livermore Laboratories in California, a government-industry cooperative program, provides outplacement counseling for employees at all levels; it includes a resource facility, counseling services, and job campaign assistance.[4] A unique element of the Livermore program is its "trainer of trainers" program where selected personnel receive special training to assist others on the job campaign trail.

The Pfizer case study in staff reduction[5] is another example. An outplacement center was established to serve as a "command post" for the 250 employees involved in outplacement. It provided a suite of offices in which they could work. They had access to a staff of counselors, psychologists, and trainers. The resource center was near but apart from the main manufacturing facility, contained voluminous reference materials for searching out jobs, and had resources for telephoning and photocopying. It was the locale for special seminars and workshops on job campaigns.

One measure of effectiveness of this kind of resource center is the outcome of the Pfizer experiment. The goal was that 90 percent of the candidates who used the center be in new positions within ninety days. Approximately 95 percent achieved this goal. Families and the local community looked favorably upon this management effort; the number of lawsuits filed by terminated employees was reduced to zero; most of the new positions paid more than the candidates' previous jobs; the cost of potential unemployment insurance premiums was reduced by approximately 60 percent. The general conclusion, aside from consideration of human values, was that the program cost only a fraction of what the potential cost of unemployment and legal settlements would have been without it.

Citicorp[6] established an outplacement program in a time of considerable transition in banking. These industry changes resulted in many personnel shifts and a recognition of the need for outplacement counseling. The staff of two counselors and a secretary provided counseling to about seventy-five candidates a year and provided consulting services to line managers on how to conduct termination interviews. In addition the counselors evaluated and recommended outplacement firms to branches in other cities. Citibank has found their program to be cost effective and successful in human terms since all of their candidates have been satisfactorily placed, with an average increase in income of 24 percent.

Sometimes universities find themselves in a position to terminate professional employees, some with long tenure. An example of how outplacement is conducted in this setting is Michigan State University, which was faced with terminating 108 tenured professors. A fund was provided to offer programs of counseling assistance and severance pay.[7] The severance options included offers to leave the university with two years pay or work the following year and leave with eighteen months pay. Most professors took advantage of some aspect of the outplacement program. Another example is the University of Washington which, under a joint task force of the Faculty Senate and the administrative officers, established a pilot program of counseling assistance to faculty members facing termination. In addition to the usual assistance in the form of retirement and severance benefits, a fund was established to support career counseling under contract with outside career counseling agencies.

THE OUTPLACEMENT PROCESS

An overview of the outplacement counseling process is presented in Figure 1. Except for Corporate Planning and Negotiating for Services, all stages apply to counseling performed either by internal or external outplacement consultants. The purpose of Figure 1 is to give a general picture of the flow of stages from termination, through counseling and placement, to final reporting of outcomes. The definitions and detailed explanations of functions in each self-descriptive heading are presented in succeeding chapters. In this chapter we cover the first stage: Corporate planning and negotiating contracts for services.

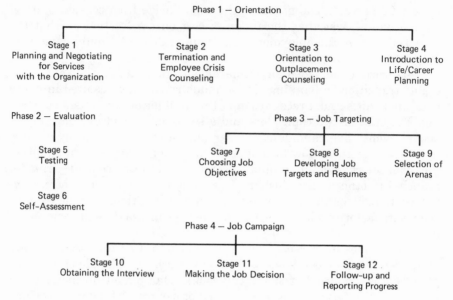

FIGURE 1   The outplacement counseling process

The Outplacement Contract Considerations

The fees for counseling service are paid by the corporation, but a contract for the outplacement counseling relationship is made between the counselor and the terminated candidate. The counselor must be satisfied that the candidate is motivated to work toward job targets. Similarly, the candidate must be satisfied with the way that the counselor manages the counseling process. There is a very fine balance of responsibility between counselor and candidate and between counselor and corporation. The counselor is accountable both to the candidate and to the organization.

The counselor's responsibility includes making monthly reports to the corporation on the progress of the candidate through the outplacement process, but the reports do not reveal any confidential personal exchanges between the counselor and the candidate. The counselor's responsibility to the organization includes the commitment to stay with the candidate until the candidate is placed, to make monthly progress reports, and to report the candidate's time and place of employment. The counselor's professional responsibilities to the candidate include career counseling, emotional support during the posttermination period, visible referral to other professionals, and a long-term, stable relationship that will facilitate the candidate's growth in self-esteem and coping skills.

The Best Placement Fit

Another unique characteristic of outplacement counseling is that sometimes it leads to consideration of up, down, or lateral placement with an enrichment effect for both the employer and the manager or employee. The outplacement counselor sometimes is, prior to the termination, engaged as an inplacement counselor by a corporation to assess a candidate's potential for other positions. Then, if the decision is made to offer an outplacement, the corporation can explain to the candidate that it has attempted to find the best fit within the corporation through inplacement counseling. In other words, the inplacement counselor, the corporation, and the candidate work very closely together to make sure that the candidate is satisfied with the way his or her life and work are progressing. When such counseling produces no better "fit" in the organization, and termination is determined to be the next step, then the counselor helps the candidate to understand and accept the reasons for termination. He or she helps the candidate to make any necessary personal changes, and then to get on with the career planning or retraining leading to the best possible placement outside the corporation.

The point of this book is to present a counseling process that can work for retraining or terminating employees. Our recent experience with approximately 300 candidates from fifty corporations has demonstrated that this process builds self-esteem and leads to effective life/work planning.

Outplacement Services in Organizational Development

Outplacement counseling is an aspect of organizational development that is concerned with transitions in the system and improving the functional capacity of the corporation. Some organizations consider outplacement services as part of compensation and benefits in personnel departments. Others place these services under training. Nevertheless, organizations look to their personnel departments when they have decided to dismiss employees, because of possible legal implications and because compensation and benefits are closely allied to termination. Outplacement counselors like to think of themselves as part of human resources management, since both the organization and the terminated employee tend to become more productive following the outplacement process.

Outplacement and Life Planning

Outplacement counseling focuses on the fine balance between life values and work goals. In this context, outplacement counseling is an aspect of life planning. In fact, outplacement counseling gives candidates, perhaps for the first time, an opportunity to look at what has happened in their immediate careers and in their lives in general. Thus, outplacement counselors, first of all, are counselors to the candidates, and secondly, act as organizational development consultants. Outplacement counselors, whether in-house or external consultants, perform a valuable service to organizations through providing feedback on personnel policies and procedures that led to the decision to terminate. The outplacement counseling procedures described in the following chapters flow from this life planning model. The same steps with the major exception of Phase 1, "Orientation," are employed for inplacement counseling.

It is unwise to keep a dissatisfied employee on the payroll. In our experience, almost every terminated employee had been disenchanted for at least six months or longer prior to being terminated. In some cases, they had severely criticized the organization—both in-house and in the community.

Outplacement of Mid-Management and Upper-Level Executives

There is a difference between mid-management and executive levels of outplacement counseling. Corporations themselves are assuming the task of counseling personnel in technical, lower-management, and non-exempt positions through their own career resource centers. Properly performed executive outplacement, however, is best accomplished by outside professionals since it is difficult for lower-level managers to counsel their superiors.

Our experience with higher-level executives is that they tend to work rapidly through the outplacement planning process. Then they will take additional months searching for the "right" position. For example, they work hard through the stage of writing a résumé; then they let it be known that they are "available." Some managers want more immediate placement and they may seek a search firm immediately rather than undertake outplacement counseling. Many managers do not feel the need for elaborate self-assessment. If they are facing a mid-life crisis, however, and are considering a major change of career, then outplacement counseling is considered essential.

Though most executives feel they probably want to obtain a new position in the same field as their last employment, there are a few who perceive the dismissal as an opportunity for a major transition to a new career or lifestyle. This option takes time to exercise, especially if it is likely to have few of the former fringe benefits that made the executive life attractive and meaningful.

All of our candidates complete an activity called "my almost impossible dream," in which they write about the activity that they have always wanted to do. A candidate, for example, decided that he had always wanted to be in business for himself as a handyman—quite a switch from his previous executive position. He established a semi-retirement position at age fifty-five, and then made himself available to elderly people of the community. At last report, he was having a very satisfying time and was making a good living. A college president, in assessment tests and counseling, discovered that he had a great interest in alternative futures as well as traditional modes of thinking and acting. The counselor had observed that the candidate's interest in the future tended to point to an interest in history. This candidate decided during the counseling that he should look carefully at a job as director of a historical museum. An industrial museum directorship opened at the time he was looking for a change of career. He applied for the position and got the job. The position fit his personal needs nicely since it did not require changing location. It met his financial requirements as well. He has been happy and can scarcely believe that "I get paid for something that is so much fun."

In another example, a candidate said that he wanted to do line work rather than be a staff consultant. He set his course on becoming a combination marketer/finance vice president of a corporation. He studied five corporations very carefully—read their brochures, studied their profit and loss statements, and collected local information on their operations. He then interviewed executives at each of the five corporations, pointing out places in the corporate structures of each where he could be used. He literally made a job for himself in these corporations. Each one offered him a position! He had given them a salary requirement 50 percent higher than he had been earning as a consultant, and most of the five offered him that amount. He chose one that would fit his work model best and became a vice-president/marketer/financial analyst at 60 percent more income—a well-paid dream come true.

Planning and Negotiating for Outplacement Counseling Services: Stage 1

When planning the outplacement counseling process and negotiating a contract for services, the corporation must consider the following:

Severance pay. Severance pay should cover three to six months. Less than three months can be interpreted to mean that the candidate is not well regarded and eligibility for counseling is questionable. A pay period of more than six months does not give the candidate sufficient motivation to work rapidly and conscientiously on the outplacement planning tasks.

Termination procedure. The contract should contain agreements to advise company personnel on termination strategies and methods. For example, interviewers need to be trained so that the termination interview is brief and simple and does not become an occasion for argumentation and bargaining. If the interviewer seems to be apologizing, the candidate is inclined to consider the corporation and the interviewer as adversaries. A trained interviewer can accomplish the termination in two to five minutes, including specific data about severance and benefits. Details are presented in Chapter 2.

Candidate files. Outplacement counselors need information from the candidate's personnel file—work record, performance appraisals, and relevant data as to why the candidate is being terminated. Access to this data file must be assured in the agreement.

Corporate communication. So that communication is consistent and regular, one person should represent the outplacement counseling firm with the corporation. The first forty-eight hours after termination are particularly important. This procedural policy helps to keep the candidate's relationship with the corporation clear and positive, and helps the outplacement counseling firm launch the candidate on a productive and troublefree path.

Fee Negotiations

An outplacement counselor's planning and negotiating contracts for services with an organization usually involves establishing the fee and determining extended service costs, such as secretarial, entertainment, or travel. Fees usually range from 10 to 20 percent of the candidate's annual earnings (which includes salary, bonus, and commissions). In addition, secretarial expenses ranging from $100 to $1500, incidental travel, and entertainment expenses are negotiated as the situation calls for.

While the external outplacement counselor remains at the disposal of candidates until they are satisfactorily placed, the counselor is available to the corporation during this time to clear up any misunderstandings about work with the candidates. This personal contact also tends to ⹁ the organization's confidence in the credibility of the outplacement coun seling service.

CORPORATE GOALS
FOR OUTPLACEMENT COUNSELING

Outplacement counseling is a service designed to accomplish specific organizational objectives. All are focused on cost savings, although it is difficult to demonstrate the cost-benefit ratios of some goals, such as community good will and the image of a caring organization. Some of these goals for the corporation are

- Reduce costs for unneeded personnel,
- Enhance a community and industrywide image of an organization that cares about people,
- Improve productivity through elimination of outdated or overpromoted personnel,
- Maintain in-house morale,
- Assist organizations to face difficult issues around affirmative action, retirement, and personality conflicts,
- Help organizations to cope with "corporate guilt,"
- Save unemployment taxes,
- Enable candidates to get "unstuck" from inappropriate job placements,
- Assist with corporate reductions and mergers.

The following elaborates on these reasons why an organization needs outplacement counseling services.

Reduce Costs for Unneeded
Personnel

Many corporations terminate personnel in an economic recession. Morin and Yorks estimate that in their experience about 10 percent of terminations are due to reorganizations or cutbacks.[8] Often, unions will help find new positions for terminated nonexempt hourly personnel, while outplacement counseling firms help management.

The pulp and paper, timber, and auto industries in the early 1980s were examples of large-scale retrenchment due to a declining economy and reduced profits. When corporations in such circumstances survey their employees to effect a reduction in force, they might consider group outplacement counseling in which the corporation does some of the assessment and guiding of the terminated employees, and an outside firm does selected phases of the counseling to supplement the organization's efforts.

Recessions bring nonproducers to the attention of top executives. These shelf sitters are retained even though they have been passed over for promotion and career development in the organization. The costs of keeping such people on, year after year, exceed the price of outplacement counseling and a few months of severance benefits. While a high rate of terminations in an organization raises morale problems and questions about company policy, there are times when every organization faces the necessity of terminating unproductive or unneeded personnel.

Enhance Community
and Industrywide Images

Organizations are looking for dollar savings; but they are also looking at the employee and public images of the corporation. Furthermore, as outplacement counseling becomes more popular, executives are requiring that outplacement counseling be one of the benefits in their contracts. When executives are terminated and not offered outplacement counseling, they may ask for counseling by an outplacement specialist. The corporation would do well to offer this benefit to create an image of being a caring organization that does not heartlessly dump its people on the street. Word on the humane or inhumane quality of the termination procedure and the benefits package spreads fast in the recruiting community and industry networks.

Improve Productivity
Through Elimination
of Obsolete or Overpromoted
Personnel

A common personnel problem is how to maintain employee productivity under conditions of rapid technological or market change. If employees are unable or reluctant to improve their performances, the corporation can terminate, transfer, or retrain them. In any case, the employee's self-esteem is jeopardized.

The goal of outplacement counseling is to help solve the organization's productivity problems as well as to protect and maintain the employee's self-esteem. This is illustrated by Harry S. His sales approaches had become increasingly outdated for the last five years, and his sales were dropping consistently. His superiors judged that he probably could function better in internal sales, but no suitable in-house position existed. He was offered training in other positions, but he persisted in his choice of external sales. He just could not see himself in any other role. So he was terminated and referred for outplacement counseling. Harry took this action very hard, but the counselor was able to support him through this adjustment process. Through vocational testing and counseling the counselor enabled him to see how he could transfer his skills and how he probably could do better as an in-house sales manager. After his self-esteem was stabilized through counseling and interview training, he found such a position in a medium-sized heavy equipment company.

Bob S., in another example, had been promoted to chief engineer, and then demoted to project engineer in a move known in business as being "put on the shelf." Now he was thought to be underqualified even for project engineer and was gaining a reputation as a misfit. Since there was no suitable in-house solution to accommodate Bob, he was terminated and offered outplacement counseling. He has since become a successful entrepreneur in his own engineering firm, where he takes on contracts within his sphere of competence and interest.

Low productivity is often due to employee obsolescence or unwillingness to grow on the job. Mary B., for example, did not demonstrate potential for increasing her productivity. She had been offered opportunities for job enrichment in her present position as research director, but she seldom took advantage of them. She was openly critical of the company and her supervisors. She became increasingly isolated from co-workers. Her performance decreased steadily to the point of chronic stagnation and obsolescence. She was terminated and outplacement counseling was the option selected. After extended counseling on her personal problems, career planning, and skills training, she took a position in product development in an overseas plant of a multinational corporation.

Mike R., a middle-aged technician who could no longer produce because of his obsolete technical skills, decided he would not put out the extra effort to grow on the job, even though he had many ideas on how to improve the company. It became an issue of his opinions versus the demands of his superior. Mike was determined to prove to his boss that his ideas had merit. He became negative in meetings and resisted his superiors at every opportunity. The inevitable happened—Mike was dismissed. The answer to Mike's future came in outplacement counseling. During his self-examination, he became more aware of the basis for his negative attitudes and reduced his stubborn behavior. He turned this negative trait into a positive, strong, decision-making competency. The assessment data and counseling supported Mike's plan to try management as a career goal.

Occasionally, personnel are promoted from positions where they have been productive to other executive levels where they do not perform as well. This condition is an example of the "Peter Principle"[9] in operation. It is very frustrating for organizations when they cannot help these people to develop their executive ability, and yet they find it awkward to suggest down placement; therefore, outplacement counseling becomes a strong option. For example, Jerry O. was wrongly placed above his capacity three years ago as a senior vice-president. He had not been productive in this position for the last eighteen months. Since no one wanted him at lower levels, and since there was no place upward, he was outplaced. This action was a shock to Jerry. Yet the outplacement counselor helped him to maintain his self-esteem and to find a new job where he could apply his former skills in a lesser position with another corporation.

Maintain In-House Morale

No matter how well the terminating process is handled, fear spreads rapidly in the office and the usual employee response is one of surprise and anxious speculation that "I may be next." Office morale is jeopardized, especially when the reasons for dismissal are not apparent to the employee's coworkers. The availability of outplacement counseling conveys to these coworkers a caring concern for satisfactory placement of the terminated employee.

This personal interest is illustrated in Dave T.'s case. The office manager was concerned about Dave, a fifty-five-year-old computer division employee of twenty-eight years. Dave had not kept up with the latest technology and he was becoming increasingly inefficient, irritable, and uncooperative. Yet, his office colleagues liked Dave. The office manager did not know what to do. The organization finally chose to offer outplacement counseling to Dave so that he could decide whether to take a lesser job offered inside the corporation or to seek an outside job. After two months of counseling, he chose to accept a lower-level job within the organization. His performance and self-esteem improved immediately. Dave smiled more, and he attended office parties again. He felt like part of the team in the new lower-level job even though the move cost him several thousand dollars in salary. Office morale increased noticeably. Had this loyal fifty-five-year-old employee with twenty-eight years of service been terminated without an offer of outplacement counseling, office morale could have plummeted, even though there was sufficient documentation from performance appraisals to demonstrate Dave's ineffectiveness. This was quite a contrast with a previous situation in which the organization had on its hands a million dollar lawsuit for what the dismissed employee termed unjust termination.

Assist Organizations in Facing Potentially Troublesome Issues

Examples of such issues are possible accusations of age, minority, or sex discrimination. Recently, cases of "reverse" age discrimination have appeared. One terminated thirty-six-year-old employee was advised by his state human rights commission to file suit for reverse age discrimination for being fired while under age forty. Age discrimination is a common claim for those inclined to be litigious. Most employees, however, do not want to expend the energy or money required to sue—particularly if they are in the outplacement process and being counseled to find a new life in a creative, practical way.

Some candidates take the opportunity when they are terminated to find new directions for their lives through outplacement counseling. For example, where they may have taken a job as administrative assistant, they now look for opportunities in marketing or personnel. Where they may have been in personnel, they now seek sales, or, in some cases, production work. In other words, outplacement counseling enables candidates to take a fresh look at themselves in a nonthreatening and helpful atmosphere. The performance ratings of Martha J., a twenty-seven-year-old woman, declined the past year and a half. She assessed herself as "on the verge of burnout." Her termination came as no surprise. In counseling she explored many alternatives. She was excited to find that although she had been in personnel for the last six years, she had competencies in other areas, including mechanical skills. In addition, she had an appealing personality. She decided to try selling in technical services, and she expressed gratitude to the corporation for offering outplacement counseling to find this new career direction.

Personality conflicts, policy and procedure, or competition for promotion may lead to the need for outplacement counseling. Personality and policies conflict, rather than inadequate performance, is, in our experience, the main reason for termination among executive-level personnel. Mel S., a production manager, had been in a race to the finish for the presidency of a small corporation. His competitor, Mark B., the marketing vice-president, won out. Mel differed greatly from Mark in temperament and outlook, and had been in constant conflict with Mark during the past three years. One of Mark's first tasks was to initiate termination proceedings against Mel for lack of "team spirit." Mark gave him six months' severance pay and offered outplacement counseling, which he accepted. Within six months Mel was employed as a production manager in another city.

Help Organizations Cope with "Corporate Guilt"

There are claims that outplacement counseling helps corporations to get rid of their guilt about dismissing capable people or people who were retained too long. An example of corporate guilt emerged while discussing John V., an employee of twenty-six years. John was being fired for his low performance of job functions and his inability to adapt to new procedures. There was a consensus that he should have been terminated twenty-five years ago and that he was mistakenly kept on at a low salary year after year. Outplacement counseling was offered as a way of helping him cope with the adjustments of early retirement and to find suitable work until he became eligible for social security benefits.

Save Unemployment Taxes

Technically, an employee may file for unemployment benefits immediately after severance payment stops. If the termination is accompanied by a cash severance benefit, then that employee will not only have the cash but also unemployment insurance payments later. Some companies deduct unemployment payments from severance pay. If the monthly severance pay and benefits are satisfactory, terminated managers and upper-level executives tend not to apply for unemployment benefits. But with nonexempt employees we have another picture. In Goodrich Corporation's reemployment program,[10] for example, its terminated employees are put through outplacement counseling, and the corporation has experienced extensive savings. Unemployment payments have decreased when the terminated employees are placed earlier than they would have been placed had they not been given this counseling help.

Enable Candidates to Get "Unstuck" from Situations Where They Were Misfits

You might hear managers saying, "It's not working," which means that they tried many ways to help the terminated employee find a way to succeed in the corporation. Finally, they gave up the attempt to get a proper management fit. Ray O., a forty-two-year-old marketing executive, said, "I knew for a long time that I wasn't producing and that I should have been fired two years ago. Better yet, I should have quit and taken a new look at myself—gotten into something else—but then I didn't have the guts." Most terminated employees consider outplacement counseling an opportunity to take a new look at themselves; many even change careers. About 25 percent of our candidates find positions in something they have always dreamed of doing.

Assist with Corporate
Reductions and Mergers

Economic pressures generate many organizational changes. Some are mergers that were unheard of in previous years—a bank takes over the assets and liabilities of a savings and loan association; a retail chain takes over an investment company; a management development company undertakes a major reshuffling of its executives and in the process, two out of the ten are released; a major electronics firm decides to emphasize two new products, and to phase out one of its old products, and in looking over its managerial talent, the board decides that one of their executives will not fit this new goal.

Sometimes managers of merging or expanding organizations are simply too busy to hire the right person. John J. was hired five years ago to do a job that was too broad for his qualifications and personality. After examining his fit in the organization, the corporation decided to divide his job into three areas, and chose three other managers to do them. They terminated John. The company gave him good recommendations and offered outplacement counseling, which helped him to put all these events in perspective and to develop a campaign for his new position. He found a new management job at the same salary in three months.

Retraining needs in industry are acute due to technological change and retrenchment. Wallace and Sheinin,[11] writing in *USA Today*, featured U.S. Labor Department data compiled for the Congressional Budget Office on dramatic shifts in the labor force. The steady increase in white-collar jobs and the steady decrease in blue-collar jobs since 1960 have accelerated since 1980. Predictions indicate that technology could eliminate another 10 to 15 million jobs by the year 2000. It is estimated that as many as 3.6 million workers may need retraining in 1983. For many workers this means retraining for an entirely new career, such as a journeyman learning to run computerized heating and cooling systems. Steel workers are learning to install and service robots, run accounting systems, and repair computers.

Not all retraining will be in high-technology fields. Many technicians will need to retrain for service jobs, such as hotel managers. Outplacement counseling services can help workers decide on the new fields for which they are going to train. Counseling is important also since it is likely that many who retrain still will not find suitable jobs. Counselors will be challenged to stay with candidates until suitable retraining sites or likely jobs are discovered.

SUMMARY

Outplacement counseling is a service to the terminated employee and to the organization. It is a logical process of counseling through twelve stages, from negotiation for services to follow-up and reporting. Nine organizational goals can be accomplished through professional outplacement counseling. Negotiating the contract with the organization includes training on how to terminate employees, describing the services and expected outcomes for counseling, and establishing the fees to be charged.

NOTES

[1]*Wall Street Journal*, April 27, 1982, p. 1.

[2]Estimated by W. Morin and L. Yorks in *Outplacement Techniques* (New York: AMACOM, 1982), p. 5.

[3]Z. Leibowitz and N. Schlossberg, "Organizational Support Systems as Buffers to Job Loss," *Journal of Vocational Behavior,* 17 (1980), 204–17.

[4]R. Rinella, *Train the Trainer: Programs for Livermore Jobs on Outplacement Counseling*. Mimeographed report, undated.

[5]E. Silverman and S. Sass, "Applying the Outplacement Concept," *Training and Development Journal* (February 1982), pp. 70–85. A case study of the Pfizer Company experience with massive layoffs at all levels.

[6]L. Anderson Clark (Manager of Executive Outplacement, Citicorp, New York City). Address to Broke Beam Forum on Outplacement, Harvard Club, New York City, June 1981.

[7]"Michigan State Faculty Layoffs: Now 10 or fewer, not 108," *Chronicle of Higher Education* (September 23, 1981), p. 2.

[8]Morin and Yorks, *Outplacement Techniques.*

[9]The Peter Principle states that people are promoted to their highest level of incompetence. L. Peter, *The Peter Plan* (New York: Bantam, 1977).

[10]Personal Correspondence between F. Humberger and Goodrich personnel staff, January 1983.

[11]J. Wallace and R. Scheinin, "Job Market Turns Blue Collars White," *USA Today,* 8 February 1983.

2

Breaking the News:
Handling the Severance Task

"You're fired" is one of the most dreaded phrases in the English language. Jobs, to professionals, managers, and executives particularly, are more than a living; they provide status, self-image, and meaning. Terminating employees, therefore, is a distasteful task for managers and executives. Even tough managers often sweat and stammer. They also have feelings of empathy for that person, who may be a friend or coworker of long standing. Some supervisors feel guilty about inflicting such pain on others, even though they are merely agents for impersonal organizations and know that such action is necessary. Consequently, terminations are pushed to the bottom of managerial responsibilities.

Anxiety about discharging in times of retrenchment is also infectious, since the people doing the terminating feel vaguely apprehensive that they may be the next ones to go. In this chapter we will present strategies and methods for Stage 2 of outpatient counseling—termination and crisis counseling. We agree with Gallagher,[1] a management consultant, that terminations should be clear, brief, and compassionate.

TERMINATION PROCEDURES

Guidelines for Terminating Employees

- Choose the appropriate person to do the terminating and the optimum time for the interview.
- Prepare a statement of severance benefits.

- Brief the executive doing the termination interview on appropriate techniques.
- Arrange for outplacement counseling to follow immediately after the termination interview.
- Introduce the terminated employee to the outplacement counselor, who usually should be in an adjacent office.
- Allow the employee to decide, in the presence of the outplacement counselor, whether or not to accept the counseling assistance.

Choosing the appropriate person to do the terminating and the optimum time.   After the decision to terminate an employee is made, the person to do the termination interview should be chosen carefully. One dismissed manager, for example, threatened trouble because the corporate president was not the one who terminated him. "If I'm to be dumped, I want the top man to do it—not that new pipsqueak who doesn't know what he's doing." He made this feeling clear and got the outplacement counselor's concurrence to have him terminated with more dignity. The decision should be based on a thorough review and a consensus of managerial peers. We believe it is wise for the appropriate supervisor to do the terminating.

Company practices dictate whether Friday afternoon is the optimum time or whether it is preferable to wait until Monday morning. Organizations have had good experience on any day of the week, especially if there are counselors close at hand to follow up on the termination interview.

Preparing a statement of severance benefits.   The personnel department should prepare a detailed statement of benefits, such as severance pay, health care, bonuses, investment returns, and pensions. Having pension information carefully prepared in advance is crucial to a severance interview involving an early or phased retirement option. The personnel manager is usually the one to prepare a letter of termination that lists the benefits, the amounts, and when they start and stop. It is given to the employee in the severance interview, with the suggestion that any further questions be discussed with the personnel department staff.

Briefing the executive on appropriate termination technique.   An inadequate or extended dismissal process will affect the outplacement counseling process negatively. The outplacement counselor should arrange a briefing with the manager doing the terminating and the personnel manager, in which the managers brief the consultant on the background of the employee and reasons for termination. The consultant should then conduct a training session in which techniques of simulating the terminating situation are used. An agenda for such a training meeting might be as follows:

- Introductions of participants,
- Review of reasons for the employee's termination,
- Role of interviewer played by consultant,
- Role of employee taken by consultant in a simulated termination interview,
- Feedback under consultant's leadership,
- Role of interviewer played by manager, followed by feedback,
- Confirmation of time and date of the termination interview and arrangements for the consultant to take over.

The consultant takes the role of the employee after some briefing on procedures. The group has a discussion following this role exercise to glean ideas for the real interview. If the executive doing the terminating has difficulties in the simulated termination process, the consultant may take the role of the manager with the manager simulating the role of the employee. This process is repeated until everyone is comfortable. While it is not possible to rehearse the details of an impending interview precisely, a mental rehearsal of opening statements and possible directions would help. This preparation helps the interviewer to maintain control of the interview, deal with confrontations constructively, communicate understanding and compassion, and terminate the interview crisply. Each interviewer has his or her own style for performing this task.

Advanced preparation might include making a checklist for inclusions and cautions for the termination interview. Gallagher has developed a "Termination Checklist"[2] that includes the following topical considerations:

- Documentation of the proposed action,
- Approvals for proposed termination,
- Prior announcements, if necessary,
- Precautions for news leaks,
- Terms of departure (when candidates have this choice),
- Legal considerations,
- Extent and timing of public announcements,
- Candidate personal considerations,
- Planning the termination interview,
- Orderly transition of candidate's responsibilities and commitments.
- Staff considerations (candidate's assistants, secretaries, associates),

- Written confirmation of termination arrangements and severance benefits.

In the training meeting, it should be suggested that the interview be brief and specific—two to five minutes to give notice, outline conditions, and suggest next steps. Ten minutes is the outside limit in most instances. During this time the interviewer states the action taken and the facts supporting the action in a humane manner that minimizes the candidate's loss of self-esteem. If the reason is a general cutback, that is made clear. If the reason is performance, then the records need to be reviewed—but only briefly. It is assumed that the employee is aware that his or her performance has been declining. Performance appraisals must accurately reflect the achievement of assigned tasks. For example, it would be awkward to cite performance as a reason for dismissal if records consistently indicate that performance is above satisfactory.

The interviewer should convey the message that the decision was based on a careful review and that it is final. Usually reasons should not be discussed in detail, for this can lead to undesirable challenging and bargaining. It is best for the terminated employee and office morale if arrangements can be made for the person to remove personal articles and leave the premises as quickly and inconspicuously as possible. Allowing the person to remain a few days, or even hours, longer often has a destructive effect on the morale of other employees, and may postpone the former employee's final acceptance of the termination.

Arranging for outplacement counseling to follow termination interview. The severance interview is scheduled at a time when the outplacement counselor can be standing by to take over. The manager brings the candidate immediately into the next office to meet the outplacement counselor or brings the counselor to where the termination takes place. The counselor will consult with the terminated employee, who is usually in shock, for one or two hours. This is the time when intense emotions are expressed. It is also the time when the counselor challenges the candidate to move forward rather than remaining stuck and depressed.

Deciding to accept outplacement counseling. It should be emphasized to the candidate that outplacement counseling is voluntary even though it is offered as part of a benefits package. Any semblance of coercion is likely to reduce the candidate's sense of personal responsibility and motivation. Rarely are offers refused, although occasionally people choose to proceed on their own, or they want some time to think about the offer. If the outplacement counselor is from an outside firm, the usual practice is to charge no fee if the terminated employee chooses not to become a candidate.

It is useful for the corporation to provide the outplacement counselor with copies of all relevant correspondence, candidate work record, performance appraisals, and notices of termination, which the counselor treats confidentially. This information helps the outplacement counselor to understand what agreements were negotiated and why the employee was terminated, and to decide how close the counselor's contact with the corporation should be in those first crucial weeks of counseling.

Pitfalls in the Firing Procedure

Some common organizational errors we have discovered in the termination process just described are

- Benefits are not clearly outlined in writing.
- The wrong person is chosen to do the terminating.
- Lawsuits are not anticipated.
- Cause of dismissal is not made unequivocal and clear.
- Spouse reactions are not considered.
- Plans are not made to respond to possible severe emotional reactions.
- The effects on remaining employees are not adequately considered.

Benefits not clearly outlined in writing.   Failing to have the benefits clearly spelled out undermines the candidate's confidence in the process and generates resentment. One candidate refused to be terminated because his supervisor simply "waved some papers in front of me."

The wrong person chosen to do the terminating.   Failing to choose the most appropriate person to conduct the termination interview can lead to trouble, as will be illustrated in the next section of this chapter.

Failure to anticipate lawsuits.   Failing to consider possible claims under the Equal Employment Opportunity Commission could be a costly error. Age discrimination is only one concern. All possible scenarios should be rehearsed and the affirmative action office should be consulted prior to the decision to terminate. Executives of one corporation were planning to dismiss a fifty-five-year-old man who was not performing up to the requirements of his newest promotion. They were reminded of a previous two-million-dollar lawsuit alleging discrimination. They met with the affirmative action officer and the outplacement counselor to choose the most prudent option among out-, lateral-, or downplacement possibilities.

Failure to make cause of termination unequivocal and clear. The organization should be adequately prepared for the consequences of an employee challenge that the termination was unjust. The following case illustrates the result of unclear reasons for termination. Darrel J. was told on April 2 that he was through as of April 3. He was president of a corporate plant and claimed he had no indication that such an abrupt action was in the making. He had a bonus and profit-sharing returns coming. More than 150 employees were depending on him for daily decisions. He thought he was doing a good job. He claimed he had always run his group in a logical and consistent style. The terminating was done by a new and young corporation vice-president who did not know the operation of this particular plant well. It appeared the vice-president made an arbitrary decision to remove certain people with whom he could not work, and this president of seventeen years was the first to go. He threatened a lawsuit, and in the meantime had started a competitive plant. Within three years the plant in the vice-president's group had to shut down, due for the most part to the candidate's competitive plant. If there are any doubts about the justification for or process of termination, legal clearance should be obtained before terminating.

Spouse reactions not considered. Potential trouble from a spouse's anger may not be considered. Spouses' attitudes often are the keys to effective outplacement counseling. One woman, for example, was angry at her husband when she learned that he had been terminated. She asked, "When are you going to keep a job longer than ten years?" Most wives are not this hard on their husbands, however, and instead direct their anger at the corporation. Usually this feeling results from a long history of the husband's nightly complaint about the awful people, the difficult markets, and unfair practices. Therefore, the spouse gets an impression that the corporation is at fault in the termination.

In many instances the spouse's anger influences the employee's negative attitudes about the counseling process. This condition has demotivated more than one candidate. It often happens in the middle of the process, just before the candidate is to go into the job market. Thus, the spouse may unknowingly reinforce the candidate's low self-esteem at the very time that self-esteem is most needed.

Candidates should be urged to level with their spouses about their terminations and their feelings, since part of the spouse's negative reaction is due to the vague and evasive manner of the candidate. It is difficult for candidates to explain forthrightly why they left. They are under great pressure to explain their terminations in ways that protect their self-respect.

In the early stages of outplacement counseling, the spouse's attitude is discussed and much negative feeling is dissipated. While spouse reaction cannot always be predicted at the time of the termination interview, the counselor should be alert to indications from the candidate about how the spouse is reacting. Gossip by disgruntled spouses can tarnish a company's reputation for fairness and as a desirable place to work.

No planning for possible severe emotional reactions. Emotional breakdown after termination is a remote, but ever-present, possibility. The process may be so traumatic that a predisposition to severe emotional breakdown may surface. This may take the form of a hysterical reaction, manifested by weeping and declarations of helplessness, intense anger, and threats of retribution; or severe depression and self-reproach. In an extreme example, a candidate in a psychotic episode ran through town screaming that Jesus was on his way to condemn the corporation. He was intercepted by the counselor who alerted mental health professionals. They helped him into protective custody in a hospital. In another instance a young woman—pregnant a second time, divorced, and under constant criticism from her parents—found that being terminated strained her coping capacities beyond their limits.

While organizations cannot be held responsible for these reactions and cannot base their termination policies on likely effects on employees, those conducting termination interviews should be prepared for the occasional emotional overreaction. Most employees experience the dismissal as an emotional shock, followed by alternating anger and relief, like the usual responses to loss described in Chapter 1, but their coping skills enable them to recover relatively quickly. In any case, it is desirable to avoid terminations near family anniversaries, special holidays, and promotion periods.

No planning for effects on remaining employees. The effect of termination on the remaining employees, especially the candidate's friends, can be disruptive to the organization. While little can be done to prepare an organization, unless it is a planned retrenchment, the supervisory staff should be alert to the likely aftermath of sudden termination on work teams. For example, people may leave the organization to join the terminated manager in a new enterprise. One destructive consequence is lowered productivity and morale resulting from the behavior of angry employees who stay but make disparaging remarks about the organization.

Occasionally, however, the remaining employees feel a sense of relief when a disliked person is dismissed. One terminated manager, for example, thought of his organization as a family, but he had failed to realize that a strong father has a smothering effect on family members. The "family" had mixed feelings of relief and sadness when the "father" left the group.

These suggestions on how terminations can affect work groups are cited in order to alert managers and executives to possible ripple effects.

LEGAL CONSIDERATIONS

Threats to Sue

Outplacement counselors can be helpful to the contracting organization when threats to sue emerge. If candidates give evidence of such intent, they are informed that their counseling cannot continue until the threat of a lawsuit is over. Candidates are reminded that a lawsuit or any adversarial position is contrary to the counseling emphasis, and are advised that once they have sued, it is difficult for them to be placed. A lawsuit takes considerable time and the job counseling process cannot be delayed for that long. Of course, candidates are informed that they have the privilege to sue if that is their wish. It is explained to them that counselors are neither advocates nor adversaries; rather they are moderators, enablers, and catalysts.

Sometimes it is necessary for the outplacement counselor to coordinate communication between the corporation and the candidate. In one example, the corporation had been concerned about a threatened lawsuit. After the counseling was completed and the candidate was on his next job, the corporation received a notice of human rights violation and a letter from an attorney. The corporation asked the outplacement counselor to intercede, and he agreed to discuss the legal implications of the action with the candidate. As a result, the employee decided that it was in his best interests to drop the suit.

Not all delicate legal problems are resolved as easily. One candidate, for example, was ready to sue for inadequate severance benefits. The corporation, terminating him quickly with little discussion about severance arrangements, had failed to discuss a bonus that he was to receive shortly, after a year of effective management. The issue became increasingly contentious and legal action was threatened. The counselor was instrumental in finally getting the matter worked out to the satisfaction of the candidate and the corporation.

Outplacement counseling does not, of course, guarantee that candidates will not sue. It merely makes lawsuits less likely because of the nature of the helping relationship and the fact that outplacement counseling often is construed by the candidate as an expression of corporate conscience, and as an expression of gratitude for years of valued service to the corporation. Outplacement counseling, however, should not be construed as an alternative to legal action.

Abusive Discharges

During the past ten years business organizations have moved far toward justifying discharge practices and establishing more "due process" procedures. Several celebrated court cases involving a large computer manufacturer, a prominent insurance company, and an exclusive retailing chain, have modified "abusive discharge" principles and practices. Alan Westin's survey[3] revealed that in 1982 twenty-seven states had legal precedents for looking into circumstances of involuntary terminations to see if they were abusive to the individual or against public policy.

Robert Coulsen,[4] president of the American Arbitration Association, cited the New Hampshire Supreme Court ruling that indicated that the employer's interest in running the business according to his or her best judgment must be balanced against the employee's interest in maintaining employment. A key issue is: What was promised at the time of hiring? Some courts are saying that the promise of job security or other benefits made at the time of hiring, whether in writing or not, could have the binding quality of a contract. A second issue considered by the courts is the length of time employed and the quality of job performance. A third issue and general guideline is whether the firing met the test of good faith and fairness. Other questions usually raised are: What public policy is involved? Was the firing retaliatory in any way?

A final factor bearing on employer-employee relationships in regard to termination issues is the political climate. The trend of the last few years is clearly to protect the interests of the employee when abusive firing is alleged. This policy may shift to more consideration of employer interests as foreign competition and employee rights threaten the corporation's survival.

The intent of recent court actions is not to take away an employer's right to terminate, but to insure that it is for cause. Increasingly, those causes are being defined in case law. For example, people usually cannot be terminated for private off-the-job behavior; neither can they be dismissed just prior to achieving full investiture in the company retirement fund, unless for gross cause. With increasing frequency, organizations are developing two strategies. One is to train personnel in the techniques of performance evaluation and termination procedures such that rancor and the probabilities of litigation are minimized. The second is to develop internal procedures for handling grievances. The broader implications include improved hiring and personnel management practices. For example, making the expectations for performance clear and the benefits explicit is crucial to minimizing the possibility of later misunderstandings. Regular and explicitly honest performance appraisals compared with performance expected at the time of hiring are essential to clear communication. By "regular" we mean that they be done on a quarterly basis.

Let us look at this issue from the organization's viewpoint. Its goal, whether making profits or offering nonprofit services, is to improve performance. Hence, employers are thinking about firing issues from the day the doors open. The rule is, "If you cannot perform, you will be terminated." Selection interviewing will never be perfect—the employee changes and may become unfit for the job; the organization also changes, making some personnel obsolete or superfluous.

Social policy regarding employee and employer rights and responsibilities is changing. More traditional organizations have held that it is their prerogative to decide who, when, and how to fire, and for what reasons. Consequently, some organizations terminate employees with a day's notice. Others may take three months to plan and notify the people scheduled for termination. Variables such as union rules and civil service laws can affect this timing. Public corporations have elaborate due process procedures that make termination a long and arduous process, except for top executives. Some organizations, such as universities and the military services, have tenure rules that make firing almost impossible except for gross negligence or financial emergency.

Many contradictory values and controversies are imbedded in these issues. The main implication for organizations considering employee termination, however, is to proceed with caution and obtain legal advice. Careful records with descriptive behavioral information devoid of prejudicial interpretations will become increasingly necessary to justify a dismissal.

A common cause of involuntary termination, for example, is that the person is a "misfit," a term that needs clear description in each case. How productive are these people as is evidenced by time spent and by output? How is performance defined? Do they spend longer than usual at coffee breaks and take long periods away for errands and lunch breaks? How is their productivity affected? Misfits sometimes exhibit annoying behavior such as confusing and antagonizing their coworkers. They often do not view corporate goals the same way as does the rest of the organization, and they take issue with many policies and procedures. Some misfits make chronic errors of judgment. When does this behavior—affecting office morale, productivity, and compatibility—accumulate to the point of intolerability? Personnel managers should keep records of the specifics on person, event, and time to justify a dismissal and to defend the organization in the event of legal action.

Even more difficult problems are likely to emerge with terminated managers and executives who do not fit the previous description. They are loyal and hardworking. They possess high performance ratings. Yet, the chief executive officer may, for example, think that a manager has outlived his or her usefulness to the corporation, that "fresh blood" is needed, or that reorganization is planned. In any case, the reasons sometimes can be considered vague and personal. We hear phrases like, "The chemistry was not right between us." To complicate this dismissal process, such persons considered for termination may be in the age fifty-five or older category so that local, state, and national age discrimination laws apply.

It is these sticky situations that lead to cases like George T., who spent thirty-one years with a large candy manufacturer. He reached the top ranks of management with a long record of awards, bonuses, and outstanding performance ratings. He felt good about his work and thought he would be staying until retirement. The president summoned him to inform him that his services were no longer required. George's response was, "I was stunned; so help me, I thought I was being called in to be offered another promotion." He was convinced that the causes cited for his dismissal were trivial and flimsy, and certainly did not warrant the "Friday afternoon massacre." George decided to sue, and after eight years of legal battles, won an appeals court ruling that he could sue for breach of contract.

The case of George T. is an example of one more precedent for justifying lawsuits over unreasonable firing. It is also a case that extends beyond legal issues of sex, race, or age. This case emphasizes the dramatic changes in employer-employee relationships since Bob Cratchet was employed by Ebenezer Scrooge. The legal tenet then in effect was known as "employment-at-will." This was an eighteenth-century common law concept governing master-servant relationships that, until recently, covered many employer-employee relationships.

These issues involved in the dismissal of employees are not unknown to personnel professionals. Corporate policies have been changed and departments have been established to meet Equal Employment Opportunity Commission standards. We notice that personnel managers are moving beyond this negative and legalistic approach to new concerns for human resource management.

More detailed information on legal issues may be acquired from Robert Coulsen's *The Termination Handbook*.[5] He cites the problems and solutions from both employer and employee perspectives. Our purpose here is to illustrate the outplacement counselor's consultant role in termination procedures and issues.

SUMMARY

Executives are briefed on termination procedures by the outplacement consultant who stands by ready to take over when the termination interview ends. The outplacement counselor assists the candidate with emotions caused by the termination, involves family members as needed, and begins the outplacement planning process.

The decision to terminate an employee involves many legal and procedural considerations. Occasionally, terminated employees threaten to sue. Age discrimination and termination without cause are two common legal challenges.

NOTES

[1]James Gallagher, *How to Manage the Termination Interview,* privately printed report, 1979, J. J. Gallagher Associates, Lincoln Building, 60 E. 42nd St. New York, 10017.

[2]James Gallagher, *The Termination Checklist,* privately printed report, 1980.

[3]Alan Westin's new book in process of publication, *Whistle Blowing and Dissent.* Reported on NBC Today Show, 7 September 1982.

[4]Robert Coulsen, cited in Eric and Cynthia Shuman, "How Secure Is Your Job?," *Dynamic Years,* Sept.–Oct. 1982, p. 24.

[5]Robert Coulsen, *The Termination Handbook* (New York: The Free Press, 1982).

3

The Outplacement Counselor Takes Over

QUALIFICATIONS OF AN EFFECTIVE OUTPLACEMENT COUNSELOR

Counselors must have certain qualifications whether they are in-house counselors—a personnel officer performing outplacement counseling duties, perhaps—or external consultants who specialize in outplacement counseling. As in health care, some counseling functions can and are being performed by persons without specialized academic qualifications. The in-house counselors may instruct candidates in career search methods and do some counseling. However, professional outside consultants also have special training to cope with the emotional aspects of termination as well as with some of the more technical complexities of career planning and placement. These external counselor/consultants have masters degrees from special counselor education programs, or doctorates in counseling psychology or a related behavioral science field. Their training includes motivation and human development. In-house counselors who have not had this special training should work in collaboration with a professional consultant for the protection of themselves and the candidate. External consultants often serve this consultive or collaborative function for in-house personnel performing outplacement counseling. The reason becomes apparent when we note the outplacement counselors' competencies and qualities:

- General helping skills and attitudes,
- Skills in use of career assessment instruments covering abilities, motivations, values, needs, and wants,
- Job search and job interviewing skills,

- Current knowledge of the employment market, and career trends,
- Credibility based on maturity, counseling reputation, and business knowledge,
- Ethical commitments and practices,
- Understanding of the outplacement process.

Helping Skills

Helping skills are classified into three groups: those encouraging self-understanding, those providing support and comfort, and those promoting decisive action. A brief overview of these skills is offered to illustrate competencies required in outplacement counseling. These skills are acquired under qualified supervisors in counselor education laboratories. Further study of this topic is recommended from Lawrence Brammer's *The Helping Relationship: Process and Skills.*[1]

Self-understanding. The goal of all helping relationships is to assist people to help themselves. More specific goals are those that build their self-esteem and feelings of personal power. To accomplish these goals, counselors need to listen with careful attention to the total message of the candidates, not merely to their words. Words often say the opposite from what the body says, the body usually being the more truthful messenger. For example, a candidate might say, "I'm all right," when his or her eyes are teary or brow is furrowed, displaying the real turmoil within.

An essential helping attitude is empathy—that ability to put one's self in the other's place and to see the world as that person sees it. When people feel they have been heard and understood, they are able to view themselves more objectively and to feel a greater sense of self-worth. The candidate's response, for example, is one of "I'm OK; I can do it; I will do it." Self-esteem, therefore, is built upon a self-image of being worthy, acceptable, and capable.

An especially helpful device that counselors should use to promote candidate self-understanding is questioning. Inexperienced counselors usually ask far too many questions; experienced counselors use a few incisive questions to get at the core of the problems. Some questions may be too challenging and confrontive, such as, "Why do you think you were fired?" Generally, questions beginning with "how" and "what" are preferable to "why" since "why" often leads to speculations about motives. This tactic may not be accurate or useful to the planning process. For example, if instead of asking, "Why did you leave that company?" the counselor asked, "What were the reasons for your leaving that company?" candidate evasion would be less likely. If the counselor wants to probe into feelings, then asking a "how" question may help. An example is "How did you really feel about that job?" In any case, questions should lead to the candidate's broader understanding rather than to the satisfaction of the counselor's curiosity.

Support. The second helping skill is supporting by making reassuring comments accompanied by a warm and caring attitude. The message to be communicated is, "I am with you in this moment of pain." The effect is that candidates feel less lonely, know that someone cares, and become convinced that they have the strength to go on. Support is given mainly through attitudes of caring and concern rather than through any specific verbal technique. The hand on the shoulder while the person talks often says more than words. The counselor is viewed as a trusted friend and advocate.

Action. Skillful counselors can intuitively judge when to stop listening or giving support, and when to expect people to be active in solving their problems. For example, in the first meeting with the candidates after the dismissal interview, it is important to listen to their reactions and respond to their feelings in an understanding and supportive manner. But there comes a point in the counseling process when candidates must say to themselves, "All right, feeling must be put aside for a while—I want to get on with it. Let's talk about what I can do to get another job." Outplacement counselors need to be alert to these indications that people are ready to go on to more rational, action-oriented discussions about solving their problems.

Assessment Skills

The assessment phase of the outplacement counseling process utilizes many modern psychological tests, inventories, and checklists. To apply these instruments properly in counseling takes a high level of psychological sophistication, which is usually acquired through research and measurement courses. It is possible to acquire these skills through experience and tutoring from consultants, but there are so many possibilities for mistakes and unethical use of assessment tools that time must be taken to acquire thorough knowledge of testing principles and practice.

Specific tests used in outplacement counseling are described in the next chapter. Here we emphasize the importance of having skills in statistical aspects of test construction and interpretation for each test in the counseling battery. Therefore, in-house counselors' preparation must include specific training in test interpretation skills through formal instruction or careful supervision by psychological consultants.

Observation is a counseling assessment tool also. Tests should only confirm what a perceptive counselor sees and hears. The counselor, using questions that probe reality, can uncover basic candidate strengths and limitations. In a second session, one candidate, for example, evidenced an exaggerated aim to please his spouse. He was surprised when confronted by the counselor about this behavior. The assessment instruments later confirmed this tendency to fake responses to be more attractive to others.

Job Search and Interviewing Skills

Outplacement counselors are primarily career planning specialists; they must be knowledgeable about how people choose their careers and about methods of job searching. Candidates should be taught the skills of writing letters of reference, constructing job resumes, assessing and utilizing support networks, mounting job campaigns, and participating in employment interviews. These methods are described in greater detail later.

Knowledge of the Employment Market and Career Trends

Outplacement counselors are not placement specialists, but they must know the job market and the corporate world. General familiarity with the world of work is a necessity. Counselors must know, for example, the duties of a trust officer in a bank or of a manufacturer's representative. They must be aware of trends and how the local economy affects those trends. Information on job openings and opportunities for the candidates' beginning their own businesses are part of this fund of local knowledge.

It is unrealistic to expect counselors to have encyclopedic knowledge of market conditions, but it is important for them to know sources of career information and where to go for special local information as well as for government data. Counselors may use, among other tools, the *Dictionary of Occupational Titles, Occupational Outlook Handbook,* and *Directory of Manufacturers,* as well as worker trait analyses, job descriptions, and profit and loss statements.

Although outplacement counselors do not make placements, knowledgeable counselors know how executive placement firms operate and how state departments of employment function. It is also important that they know networking operations in business, military, and governmental organizations, since so much of the job placement effort of the candidate is based on an extensive network of helpful contacts. Specialized knowledge such as unemployment compensation and rehabilitation of the disabled is helpful. Special legislation affecting older workers, such as the laws about discrimination and mandatory retirement, is an essential part of the counselor's knowledge base.

Credibility Factors

While it is important to have professional and technical skills, there are some additional characteristics that make outplacement counselors effective. Some of these qualities that build the candidate's confidence and give counselors credibility are

- Ability to motivate to action,
- Maturity,
- Managerial experience,
- Experience with personal loss,
- Reputation as a counselor,
- Certainty of their own career direction,
- Reality centeredness.

Motivation. Since getting candidates to move through the process and to persist in their job search is often a difficult task, it is important that the counselor have a strong ability to motivate people. This is manifested by persistent encouragement, being enthusiastic about the task, and keeping the candidate actively involved. Motivation to action involves keeping the discussions and plans focused on the task rather than ranging widely over irrelevant topics. Candidates often use this ploy to resist commitment and to avoid the reality of planning. Staying with the process takes strong discipline, and the counselor must be an ally to the part of the candidate's personality that wants to complete the process with maximum speed.

Maturity. Gray hair and wrinkles help to maintain the impression that the counselor is mature and competent. Marks of aging are evidence that the counselor has been "kicked around by life" too. Since many candidates in outplacement counseling are middle-aged people, counselors' credibility is enhanced if they appear to be contemporaries. For example, a fifty-year-old company executive is unlikely to give credence to the career ideas of a newly graduated psychologist, no matter how competent that counselor may be. With a mature counselor, there is less likelihood of the candidate taking the process lightly because the younger counselor lacks effectiveness.

Managerial experience.   Some managerial experience is also desirable for credibility. An appreciation of the fact that the counselor "has met a payroll too" is stronger in the business community than in other types of organizations. In addition, there is a vocabulary and a shared experience that facilitate rapport and counselor empathy. For example, it is helpful for counselors to know firsthand the kinds of pressures faced by executives of a corporation. Then there will be less need for the status games that managers play, because candidates know they cannot bluff or impress counselors who have been there and know the games too. Shared experiences in making a profit and managing an enterprise facilitate rapport, and help to get more quickly to the personality bases of problems associated with the job.

Personal loss.   While it is not essential for counselors to have been discharged at some previous time to understand what it is like, it is desirable that they have experienced severe life changes and losses in order to appreciate the devastating feelings that result from being discharged. Loss experience is also essential in order to understand more clearly the grieving process that is provoked by losing a valued job and its associated lifestyle.

Reputation as a counselor.   Word gets around quickly in organizational networks and industry underground channels about who is effective with what kinds of people. This reputation is based in part on a counselor's record of successful placements, but it depends also on certain human qualities that build confidence and make a working relationship possible. Effective outplacement counselors have reputations of being helpers.

Certainty of the counselor's own career direction.   It is controversial whether counselors must convey an attitude of certainty about their own career directions or whether it is helpful to honestly reveal the presence of career confusion and uncertainty in their personal lives. It is our opinion that counselors should be assured about the direction of their own lives and should manifest quiet confidence and satisfaction. Models have a powerful impact on people, and counselors are models of the services they are promoting. Any confusion or uncertainty about the counselor's career direction had best be handled in consultation with colleagues rather than with candidates. The counselor mentioning *personal experiences* in career planning, however, could be reassuring to candidates.

Reality Centeredness

The counselor must be able to confront candidates on many personal issues of work, family, law, and finance. Reality centeredness is a quality of being aware of and attending to what is of prime concern to the candidate at the present moment, and then dealing with the issue of greatest priority. It is a way of focusing explicitly on behavior that the candidate may not be aware of at the time. For example, a candidate who speaks about the possibilities of litigation puts the counselor on alert for legal threats that must be handled realistically. One candidate had to shorten the outplacement counseling process from the usual three or four months to four weeks because of the urgent reality of a financial loss the employee experienced just prior to termination. One candidate experienced a psychotic episode upon termination. The counselor's alertness and focus on this urgent reality resulted in immediate referral to mental health specialists for possible hospitalization. In another example, a candidate continued to receive severance pay while on a new job. He was fearful of not surviving the learning phase of the new job so he lied to his former employer about his new employment status. The counselor confronted him about this grossly unethical behavior and established a clear course of action.

Reality centeredness is the quality of the counselor being alert to what is going on at different levels of communication and then forthrightly confronting the candidate with the observation or interpretation.

Ethical Commitments
and Practices

The main ethical issue for counselors is how to juggle the dual loyalties to candidates and to the sponsoring corporation. Corporations ask for progress and outcome reports to know if their investments in candidates are justified. The general ethical guideline is to report only progress through the outplacement counseling process, and when and where the candidate was placed. Candidates understand and agree to this reporting contract, but they also understand that personal information revealed in counseling is never repeated. Even under pressure, confidential, personal data are not revealed without explicit permission of the candidate. Psychological counselors are committed to this principle of confidentiality through their subscription to the *Ethical Principles for Psychologists*.[2] This is a set of principles that reflects the current values of society and the special concerns of individuals for protection of their privacy.

The private contract counselor has ethical obligations to the corporation to carry out agreements for providing services. The contract counselor is accountable, then, to the sponsoring organization for the proper use of the outplacement counseling fee.

The counselor should inform candidates about the likely rate of obsolescence for any job considered. It might be expedient to try for a short-term fit in a job that is attractive now but is likely to be obsolete in a few years. Counselors must remain current in their knowledge about career information in order to properly advise candidates on the essential qualifications and preparation required for highly complex jobs.

Counselors also have an ethical obligation to validate the instruments and processes that are used in outplacement counseling. An important question is whether the assessment tools work as effectively as stated in the manuals for special populations of terminated employees. For example, does the Myers-Briggs type indicator describe candidates' attitudinal preference accurately enough to be useful in outplacement counseling? Humberger,[3] who has used the MBTI in outplacement counseling, studied its use with 178 candidates over a two-year period. He was interested in how accurately the MBTI results related to job characteristics and reasons for termination.

Counselors have an ethical obligation to practice their skills within their levels of competence. As in any new service field, many people are trying outplacement counseling without the proper professional qualifications. There are no licenses or certificates for being an outplacement or inplacement counselor, unless one also uses the title "psychologist." State laws regulate the title and practice of psychology. Leadership in setting standards for practice has been demonstrated by Gallagher in his "Standards of Practice for Outplacement Professionals."[4] Some of the principles for practice cited by Gallagher are

- Avoids conflicts of interest;
- Offers outplacement counseling services as a serious professional specialty, emphasizing quality;
- Respects candidates receiving service;
- Maintains broad experience and competence to speak with authority;
- Commits to candidate goals, and develops discipline to stay with the candidate until the job campaign is concluded;
- Treats confidential information with discretion.

Gallagher states also that, while he supports high standards, he has yet to see the "perfect" credentials to practice outplacement counseling.

The general qualifications cited above must be supplemented with specific knowledge about the outplacement counseling process. Skills for managing crises were designed to help the candidate cope with the shock and early stages of grieving over the job loss. These skills need to include stress management and family counseling, especially if the candidate reacts severely to the termination interview. Further information about how professionals and managers cope with crisis and the stress of unemployment is covered in H. G. Kaufman's *Professionals in Search of Work: Coping with the Stress of Job Loss and Unemployment.*[5]

OUTPLACEMENT COUNSELING BEGINS

The counselor is introduced to new candidates as soon as possible after they are terminated. If they agree to accept outplacement counseling, the process begins. Candidates also may have the option in their contracts to request a different outplacement counseling firm. They also may go into the job market alone or use whatever job search facilities that might be available through the corporation benefit package.

Assuming readiness to proceed, the counselor's first task is to allow candidates to ventilate feelings about being fired. Reactions vary. Candidates are usually shocked and dismayed. Even though they may have had some inkling that termination was imminent, they tend to react with disbelief—"How could this happen to me?" At some point in the process the counselor needs to probe for these signs that candidates may have overlooked, such as not being invited to important meetings or being cut from memo distribution lists.

Sometimes the termination is greeted with relief, as in the case of an employee who was considering early retirement but could not come to the point of filing that application for retirement.

After a period of venting feelings and settling down, the counselor explains the outplacement process. The goals of this discussion are to reestablish some of the candidate's lost self-esteem, to give information about the process, and to offer assurance of support until the candidate is placed in a new position. A contract is then made between the consultant and the candidate to continue the job or career search process. This contract includes a job target date and the date by which each step is to be achieved. It is signed by the candidate and the counselor. Completion of each step adds to the candidate's self-confidence and hope.

The goals of these early stages are to help the candidate express feelings and to prepare for the more rational stages of outplacement counseling to follow. The foundation is laid for the view that this crisis is an opportunity for growth and a new life.

A summary of procedures utilized in the early stages of outplacement counseling follows:

- Discussing feelings about being terminated,
- Managing the likely crises with supportive counseling,
- Ascertaining willingness to begin outplacement counseling,
- Explaining the outplacement counseling process,
- Negotiating the counseling contract,
- Arranging for possible counseling of spouse and family,
- Planning the daily schedule,
- Making homework assignments,
- Arranging appointments.

Personal Problems

It is desirable to explore the candidate's family situation to see if there is a need to refer the candidate to outside mental health counselors for alcoholism, emotional, or family problems.

For example, it is difficult to work on career planning with an actively alcoholic candidate. It is complicated even if the spouse is an alcoholic and the candidate is not. It is usually wise to refer the alcoholic candidate for special treatment, either concomitant with career counseling or prior to doing any serious career planning. Outplacement counselors are reluctant to work with such candidates until they reach the recovery stage because excessive use of alcohol is one of the most difficult behavior patterns to correct. Some specialists regard alcoholism as a disease; yet candidates must believe they have some control over their drinking. The recovery rate is not encouraging—estimates range up to 50 percent; employee assistance programs, however, report 70 to 80 percent recovery.[6]

Employers are cautious about alcoholics because of the enormous costs, estimated to be $25 billion annually for absenteeism and health problems. There are an estimated 10 million alcoholics in the United States; half of them are employed. Organizations are moving increasingly to in-house treatment programs. Five thousand companies now offer treatment and reemployment training through employee assistance programs that are judged to be cost effective.[7] These data are cited here to indicate the nature of the problem for the person now unemployed due to alcoholism. It is essential that affected candidates find ways to correct this problem before seeking reemployment.

The trauma of being terminated occasionally unleashes latent personality problems, precipitates depressions, intensifies feelings of job burnout, and covers all relationships with an air of tenseness and bitterness. These conditions usually interfere with rational career planning and job choice. People should be rehabilitated as much as possible in the outplacement process to give them better chance of success in their next jobs. The counselor's task is not to change the candidate's personality but to increase awareness about how certain traits may hinder future job performance.

The outplacement counselor may do some counseling on these personal problems, but it is usually wiser to refer them to a psychological or psychiatric consultant when more than six to eight hours of personal counseling are required. If candidates' problems are so severe that they require more extended psychotherapy, they are so apprised of this opinion and are encouraged to accept referral to a therapist or counselor not connected with the outplacement enterprise. The counselor suggests up to three such referrals and then lets candidates choose from among them, or allows candidates to make their own selections. The counselor helps the candidates decide whether they should continue the outplacement counseling or suspend it until the therapy progresses. The candidates are assured, however, that the outplacement counselor will stay with them until they are placed.

Crisis management. The first goal is relief of discomfort and suffering. After termination, candidates often go into a state of shock, which is experienced as numbness and pain. This is the first stage of grieving; the brain goes into "neutral," feelings become dull, and bodily activity slows. This neutral and dull condition is followed shortly by a painful outpouring of feeling—anger, fear, and general anguish. At this point candidates need considerable support from their families and from the counselor. The counselor first of all must assess the condition of the candidates and intuitively decide what is best to do at this point. Usually, support is provided by just being with them and listening to the feelings being expressed. Sometimes candidates need encouragement to express feelings they are experiencing, including permission to let go with tears or tantrums. The goals are to release feelings, maintain hope, and enhance self-esteem. Offering hope through the outplacement counseling process is helpful at this point. Further methods for understanding crises and for providing support may be found in Brammer's *The Helping Relationship*.[8]

Self-esteem. Some candidates, when facing the consequences of being terminated, direct their anger and fear at themselves. As a result, their feelings of worth plummet. While this condition is to be expected in this early stage, counselors must be prepared to help candidates bolster their self-esteem. Outlining clear steps they will be taking in counseling is helpful in building hope and optimism. Focusing on past achievements, transferable skills, needs, wants, and values also helps keep personal worth in perspective. As candidates get further into the self-evaluation and job campaign phases, their self-esteem tends to rise. Seeing their own strengths and positive traits in profile form during counseling is self-affirming. Later in the counseling process, candidates begin to reconceptualize the meaning of the transition they are experiencing. They begin to see that perhaps this experience is providing an opportunity to take a long, hard look at their lives, their goals, and their satisfactions. They begin to see this transition as a challenge and as an opportunity.

Jessie D., a twenty-six-year-old data processing clerk, was informed of her termination on the same day her husband was dismissed from another corporation. She was pressured by her family to divorce her husband and move in with them to ease the hardship of losing her job. This multiplicity of personal problems was devastating. Thanks to a supportive and caring outplacement counselor, she gained the needed self-esteem and strength to face up to her parents as well as to support her grieving husband. She grew confident that she could find a new job; this gave her husband renewed confidence to find his way. They both succeeded.

Candidates who persistently criticize themselves severely may be exhibiting a long-standing personal style that has been exaggerated during this job transition. The motives for severe self-criticism are complex. They may be rooted in feelings of inadequacy and result in the need to have constant reassurance of adequacy from others. Self-criticism may also be a method of sending messages to others that they do not want to take responsibility for themselves or that they want to remind others subtly of their authority and position. It is like the teenager who says that he is "always goofing things up," but who may actually want to avoid responsibility for achieving adequately.

Self-criticism may be a message to others not to make demands or criticisms. Regardless of cause, self-critical candidates are in pain and they usually have little awareness that they themselves are perpetuating it. When this persistent condition is observed in candidates, referral to a psychological counselor is indicated. Outplacement counselors need to distinguish among self-criticisms that are based on honest efforts to improve performance, those that result from temporary grief over loss of a job, and those that are rooted in long-standing personality problems.

Depression Management
and Coping with Grief

Any severe loss, including unemployment, results in grief. This grieving process follows predictable stages, although not always in the same order. These stages were described by Elisabeth Kübler-Ross[9] as reactions to loss of a relationship through death. Losing a job can trigger stages of experience similar to those precipitated by a death.

First, people experience shock and disbelief. They sometimes feel stunned, even shattered—as if their world were coming to an end. Often this shock is accompanied by a denial—"No, it can't be true." Denial sometimes is expressed as a withdrawal into their own shell or pretending they are not shocked or disappointed. This denial mechanism causes problems during the termination interview, also, since candidates distort or do not hear what the interviewer is saying.

The second stage is marked by strong, active emotion—sometimes sadness, but more likely anger. Occasionally, the immediate feeling is one of momentary pleasure or relief from a frustrating and unrewarding job, but this feeling quickly turns to anger when it is realized that the termination was not on the employee's terms.

The third stage is characterized by deepening sadness—even depression. This period may last several days or weeks and is accompanied by a feeling of lowered self-worth. Outplacement counseling deals initially with these grief reactions before plunging ahead with planning for a new job or moving toward a new career.

The fourth stage is movement toward change and the consideration of new job possibilities. Self-esteem improves, optimism prevails, and motivation for planning and deciding on a job campaign is evident.

For some people, these stages may be so subtle as to be hardly noticed and they may last only a few days. For others, they may be wrenching and disruptive. Some stages may stretch out for months before the person is ready to consider alternatives and act decisively on a job search. Sometimes candidates will start counseling fairly energetically and then hit a slump six to eight weeks later. The practical implication of these facts is that counselors need to determine accurately when candidates are ready to move into the planning and campaign phases and how much attention must be given to the grieving process.

At times during this grieving process, the terminated employee becomes disturbed because the pressures are so great. Some candidates, for example, have gone back to the corporation in deep anger and engaged in fights with the people who had fired them. One candidate, for example, said angrily, "I have thought of using my 357 Magnum to kill my boss." The counselor responded paradoxically, "That should do the job." Candidate and counselor laughed together. This use of paradoxical humor and acknowledgment of his anger brought some perspective to the candidate's feelings and cleared the way to go on with his career counseling. There have also been candidates who have taken out their anger and disappointment on their families in a physical way. Spouse and child abuse tend to increase during periods of high unemployment.[10] Emotions often become strong and uncontrollable when jobs are lost.

Candidates need to be assured that experiencing frequent bouts of depression as counseling proceeds is a normal part of the grieving process.

The sadness results from the numerous losses associated with being terminated from a job of long tenure. Psychologists call this normal sadness a "reactive depression." It is only when the depression becomes chronic or so severe that it interferes with daily functions and relationships, that referral for possible medication or residential treatment should be considered.

The outplacement or inplacement counselor must be alert to the day-to-day changes in candidates and be observant of any indications that the candidates are considering suicide. If such is the case, consultation with professional colleagues is indicated and the candidates' families and health support systems may need to be alerted. The ethical code, previously described, to which the counselor subscribes requires that such prudent action be taken when candidates threaten suicide.

Involving the Spouse

During the orientation, the counselor suggests that spouses be invited into the process—partly to orient them to what is going on and to make them partners, but also because they are significant persons to the candidates and influence them profoundly. Experienced outplacement counselors claim that almost half of the families of terminated managers accuse them of failure rather than offering them support.[11] Family plans for children's education and paying the mortgage are suddenly in jeopardy. Anxiety and anger are normal family responses.

Sometimes spouses attend all counseling sessions, although it is most common for them to come only for a time or two during the initial counseling stage. The spouse often does not understand the process, and may unknowingly become less supportive as the months go by without a job for the candidate. The counselor may invite the couple to dinner, sometimes including the counselor's spouse.

A spouse is usually a key factor in sustaining the candidate's motivation to keep at the process, maintaining his or her self-esteem and providing a generally stable and routine environment. One spouse, for example, was invited to join in the process when the candidate was procrastinating. When she saw his cavalier attitude on the interview videotape, she marched him into the job market, saying, "Get going, we need food now!" Questions regarding how to tell the children should be considered jointly. One couple never did tell the children until their father found his next position.

Sometimes spouses need special counseling to take care of their own needs during this trying transition. Spouses need help in venting their anger constructively. After listening to the candidates criticize the corporation daily, they build a reservoir of resentment just waiting to spill out to reporters, lawyers, and gossipy neighbors. Lawsuits often start with the angry spouse.

Usually spouses are grateful later for the opportunity to examine their values and plan new lives together. One spouse, for example, returned to Henry's former boss and said, "This was the best thing that ever happened to Henry; he was unhappy for the last thirteen years."

ORIENTATION TO OUTPLACEMENT COUNSELING

Explaining what outplacement counseling entails and building realistic expectations are the two most important goals of Stage 3 in the outplacement counseling process, Orientation to Outplacement Counseling. To carry out the process described below candidates need a plan and a guidebook to keep them on track toward their outplacement counseling goals. Humberger's *Your Career Plan*[12] is an example of such a plan book introduced in the orientation phase of counseling.

Time Commitments

Candidates often spend up to 300 hours working on the process from entry to job placement. Counselors spend from thirty to sixty-five hours for each candidate. Thus, candidates usually spend five times more hours than do the counselors. The higher the executive rank, the longer it takes to find the right job. For example, it is not unusual that a top executive will wait for that right job situation for as long as a year.

Counselors and candidates should keep daily records on hours devoted to the process, which ends when candidates are successful in their job interviews. A key task of the outplacement counselor is to monitor candidates and to keep them working at an optimum pace.

A summary of time commitments follows:

- Orientation to outplacement counseling (up to five hours for counselor and candidate).
- Self-assessment (up to sixty hours for candidate; up to twenty hours for counselor).
- Self-marketing preparation and job targeting (up to forty hours for candidate; up to ten hours for counselor).
- Job campaign and interview training (100 to 200 hours for candidate, five to thirty hours for counselor).
- Job decision and acceptance (up to five hours for the candidate).

Self-Defeating Tendencies

When candidates understand what is to be expected, they must be cautioned about several self-defeating tendencies in the early stage:

- Rushing into the job search,
- Expecting immediate results,
- Taking the first job offer,
- Rushing to seek help from friends and connections,
- Placing ads before planning is well along,
- Escaping from the planning tasks,
- Dwelling on the past,
- Blaming self,
- Accusing the organization,
- Provoking arguments with spouse,
- Rushing to employment agencies or search firms.

Rushing into the job search.   It is normal for candidates to feel frustrated, angry, confused, and fearful when they think of the job search ahead. One candidate, for example, became so immobilized that she could not write. It is important for the candidate to know that, as the process continues, these feelings will subside and be replaced by confidence, self-worthiness, and optimism. Many talents are discovered in this search, contributing to these good feelings.

Expecting immediate results.   It is important for candidates to realize that counseling and the job search take time and are not easy tasks. It usually takes a minimum of three months to find the right job that fits the candidate. One candidate, for example, rushed into the job market after six weeks, thus aborting the program. He was back six months later after leaving that poorly considered position.

Taking the first job offer.   Counseling provides an opportunity for candidates to find themselves at this time of crisis. When candidates say they have a job waiting, counselors should do some confrontive reality checking. It is important that candidates take the time to engage in the in-depth self-study and to take advantage of professional help; therefore, it is important that they get far enough into the process to form a profile against which to place the prospective job. It takes some time also to let go of past attachments and to be open to something new so that positive outcomes can emerge from this negative experience of being discharged.

Rushing to friends and connections. When candidates are anxious, there is a tendency to seek friends and network contacts immediately to inquire about job leads. To do this before they are properly prepared may destroy the image that they are poised and may cut off potential avenues of job leads. One candidate, for example, was criticizing his former company as he was telling friends of his job search. He was overheard by a potential employer who disapproved of this behavior, and cut off any chances the candidate may have had with that company.

Placing newspaper or journal ads. Candidates must be made to realize that there is an optimum time in the job campaign phase when ads are appropriate, although most employers do not search personal ads.

Escaping. Escape such as going on a vacation immediately may be an activity the candidates use to avoid working on their futures. Any effort to escape this most important job of their lives will sap the energy of the candidates.

Dwelling on the past. A temptation in times of stress is to engage in "what if . . ." fantasies. "What if I had done. . . ." "What if my boss had not done. . . ." Looking backward takes energy away from the essential task of looking forward. One candidate, for example, continued to blame her coworkers for her termination. "I did well in another department. I wish they had never transferred me to those conniving people."

Blaming self. Self-blame is a waste of time and money. This kind of negative thinking makes it difficult to write the reference letter on past experiences. Candidates must come to believe that they made the best possible choices at the time. The counseling process can dispel this self-blame before it builds up and interferes with planning and action.

Arguing with spouse. There is a tendency for candidates to project blame on their spouses or to be especially touchy during this transition period. It is easy, therefore, for them to get into arguments over small issues. Spouses are under strain too and tend to be accusative and argumentative. One candidate's spouse divorced him when his immature behavior became exaggerated under the stress of his termination.

Rushing to employment agencies or "headhunters." Under the perceived pressure of finding a job, candidates are tempted to look up old executive search firm acquaintances, thinking they might immediately suggest a job. Occasionally a good job offer is solicited this way, but more likely it will be a premature choice. The agency will probably hold the candidate's résumé and do what it wants with it, rendering the job campaign out of the candidate's control. The outplacement counselor must encourage candidates to become their own search experts through a number of other methods.

Candidates who probably have managed many people over the years now have a chance to manage themselves. It is perceived as an opportunity by some candidates; sometimes they say that this career planning task was the single most challenging event in their lives. "Have faith in yourself" is the motto to be encouraged at this initial stage of counseling. Occasionally, candidates imply gratitude to their former employers for discharging them. Some have said, "I didn't have the guts to quit a bad situation," "I knew I wasn't producing," "I was looking around anyway," "I was stuck on that job," "I'm glad to be out of a bad situation."

Why Were You Terminated?

The counselor must ask candidates about the conditions leading to their terminations. Sometimes candidates volunteer this information, but most of the time the counselor must broach the subject during Stage 5— initial counseling. If the termination was strictly for reasons of job elimination, it is easier to face. If the dismissal was for lack of performance or personal conflict with peers, subordinates, or superiors, however, stated reasons are likely to be more defensive.

Discussing this subject forthrightly is important to encourage candidates to correct any deficiencies in behavior that are likely to cause difficulties on the next job, and as a prelude to interviewing. Job interviewers often ask why interviewees were discharged. Some overt behavior, such as appearance and personal hygiene, are easily correctable; more pervasive personality traits are more impervious to change. For example, one manager was terminated because women subordinates could not tolerate his offensive behavior toward them. Counseling involved months of probing and confronting to make the candidate aware of his deep hostility toward women. He was defensive at first, but he finally admitted that, "I need to think of other people's feelings."

Studies are being made that help us to understand why managers and executives are dismissed. Morgan McCall reported about "tragic flaws" of discharged executives, in research conducted with V. Jon Bentz at Sears and Roebuck.[13] These investigators found the following reasons for executive dismissal:

- Decline in business performance (manifested in a series of small setbacks and mistakes).
- Intensive, abrasive, intimidating style (leaves a trail of little problems and offended people).
- Cold, aloof, and arrogant manner (after a history of success).
- Overmanagement (did not delegate enough and became mired in detail).
- Excessive ambition (too obvious in office politicking).
- Poor staff selections.
- Inability to think strategically.
- Inability to adapt to superiors or the executive culture.
- Overdependency (the fair-haired boy is left alone when his mentor or advocate is shifted).
- Specific skill deficiencies (becomes apparent when losing a superior or colleague who has been covering for deficiencies).

These researchers found similarities between the successful survivors and the "fatally flawed"—they were very intelligent, had superb records, and were identified early as comers. The flawed executives who were later dismissed developed a style that became ineffective with people. They developed blind spots to behaviors others viewed as arrogance. The successful survivors made fewer mistakes and handled those mistakes with more grace. Some derailed executives appeared to be victims of situational changes such as mergers, conflicts, politics, and personnel shifts. Under these conditions, strengths suddenly became weaknesses and events converged to finally overcome the executive. It was not one thing but a combination of traits and events. The implications of this research for managerial candidates undergoing outplacement or inplacement counseling are obvious. This list can be used as a template to help candidates assess where they might have gone off track.

Occasionally executives will report that the reason behind their performance problems was burnout. This term is a catchall to cover progressive deterioration of performance associated with mental and physical exhaustion. The reaction is "I've had it!" High achievers, especially those in delivery of and management of human services, are vulnerable. It is a complex condition that needs to be examined in the initial stages of outplacement or inplacement counseling. Vulnerability to burnout caused by overwork, boredom, or conflict of values needs to be explored and understood. Sometimes a plateau is reached, resulting in feelings of boredom or entrapment. Preventative action must be taken so the cycle does not repeat itself on the new job. A candidate's awareness of vulnerability to burnout in the last job might suggest a different career direction.

Emotions in Outplacement
Counseling: A Summary

This chapter has dealt with two aspects of emotion in outplacement counseling—those feelings of anger, pain, and fear experienced at the time of firing, and those experienced when considering the reasons for the termination. A summary of suggestions counselors might offer to candidates follows:

- Do not panic—the outplacement process will ease anxiety.
- Express anger—the feelings of injustice, bitterness, and recrimination must be let out.
- Cope with depression—admit depressed feelings openly and get suggestions for coping.
- Take stock of assets and limitations—be objective.
- Accept the reality of the situation and of personal strengths and limitations.
- Discover real satisfactions and goals in life.
- Make this an opportunity for a learning experience instead of a painful event.
- Have faith in the process—self-regard and confidence will return and you will be stronger than before.

Contracts, Assignments,
and Appointments

The contract made between the counselor and candidate is checked frequently during the process to judge progress toward the goal of job placement. All contractual agreements on tasks and completion dates are recorded on a form "Self-Tracking the Outplacement Counseling Program" illustrated in Figure 2. Both candidate and counselor retain copies. Assignments are made at the end of each counseling session. Early in the process candidates are given a manual of forms on educational background and work history. As noted in the next chapter, there is a large battery of checklists, tests, and inventories to be completed at home as part of the self-assessment phase.

Finally, an appointment schedule is prepared to keep the momentum going. The process moves along logically except when the candidate skips or cuts a step in the tightly planned sequence. Candidates should be encouraged to make this process the central focus of their lives until they are placed satisfactorily. It is important to leave candidates with the

Candidate: _____ Address: _____ Telephone No. _____

Sponsoring Co.: _____ Sponsoring Co. Contact: _____ Telephone No. _____

Start Date: _____ Consultant: _____ Orientation Completion Date _____

Previous Salary: _____ Career Tests Estimated Date to Find New Position _____

Previous Title: _____ yes ☐ no ☐

Scheduled Date Completion Date	List of Personal ("Network")	Positive Reference Statement	Job Achievements and Accomplishments	Skills Summary	Job Objective(s)	Needs, Values, Wants	Draft of Resume(s)
	___	___	___	___	___	___	___

Scheduled Date Completion Date	Final Draft of Resume(s)	Final Draft of Broadcast Letters	Planning of Self-Marketing	Strategy and Tactics	Difficult Questions	Practice Job Interview
	___	___	___	___	___	___

Scheduled Date Completed Date	Date of First Interview	Dates Further V.T. Interview	Campaign Trail
	___	___	___

New Placement Status

Name of Company: _____   Position Accepted: _____   Salary: _____

Total Time in Outplacement Counseling Program: _____

FIGURE 2 Self-tracking the outplacement counseling program

conviction that this is their search and that the counselor is a consultant/ coach/facilitator.

SUMMARY

The outplacement counselor takes over immediately after the candidate is terminated. An orientation to the outplacement counseling process is given. The counselor is prepared to cope with the candidate's feelings of shock, grief, or relief. Together they make a plan to achieve the goals of outplacement counseling. To assist candidates to reach these goals, counselors must have skills in general counseling, crisis management, assessment, career planning, and conducting job searches. Counselors must also know when to refer candidates to specialists for more extended personal counseling. Frank discussions about reasons for the candidate's termination are conducted to identify and remove barriers to future employment.

NOTES

[1] L. M. Brammer, *The Helping Relationship: Process and Skills,* 2nd ed. (Englewood Cliffs, N.J.: Prentice-Hall, 1979). (An introduction to the skills and concepts needed by the nonprofessional helping person.)

[2] American Psychological Association, *Ethical Principles for Psychologists* (Washington, D.C.: American Psychological Association, 1981).

[3] F. Humberger. Unpublished data collected in 1980–82. For further information, write Executive Services Associates, Suite 244, Lincoln Center, Bellevue, Washington 98004.

[4] J. J. Gallagher, "Standards of Practice for Outplacement Professionals," published in *Directory of Outplacement Firms* (Fitzwilliam, N.H.: Kennedy and Kennedy, 1982).

[5] H. G. Kaufman, *Professionals in Search of Work: Coping with the Stress of Job Loss and Unemployment* (New York: Wiley, 1982). (A description of the psychological problems of job loss and unemployment among professional workers. Identifies unemployment stress and coping strategies to deal with stress.)

[6] Ibid.

[7] Ibid.

[8] Brammer, *The Helping Relationship.*

[9] E. Kübler-Ross, *Death: The Final Stage of Growth* (Englewood Cliffs, N.J.: Prentice-Hall, 1975).

[10]American Psychology Association, *Monitor,* Report of research by P. Brenner on psychological effects of unemployment, p. 2.

[11]W. Morin and L. Yorks, *Outplacement Techniques* (New York: Amacom, 1982).

[12]Frank Humberger, *Your Career Plan* (Privately printed, 1979).

[13]Morgan McCall and V. Jon Bentz of Sears. A preliminary report presented at American Psychological Association meeting, Washington, D.C., 25 August 1982. Later published as part of "What Makes a Top Executive?" by M. W. McColl and M. M. Lombardo, *Psychology Today* (1983) 22: 26–31.

4

Candidates Assess Themselves

The outplacement counseling process requires much data from the candidate. The goal is to obtain an accurate picture of the candidate's total person—values, wants, interests, skills, traits, accomplishments, and achievements. It is important to realize that this assessment is not primarily for the counselor's diagnosis and planning, but to help candidates become aware of each facet of themselves, so they can make informed choices of career and job, as well as general life style.

A second goal of the self-assessment phase is rebuilding self-esteem. When candidates discover their strengths, appreciate their achievements, and clarify their limitations, then their self-esteem rises. They are encouraged by the closer grip on reality provided by valid self-descriptive information and accurate job market data.

Following are several types of assessment categories with illustrative assessment strategies and instruments. The counselor must tailor assessment strategy and battery to the needs of each candidate and to the policies of the organization. For example, are certain types of personality tests not to be administered in certain companies? Test instruments of any type must be administered and interpreted under standard conditions prescribed in the test manuals in order to be valid.

AREAS OF ASSESSMENT

The principal areas of assessment are

- "My almost impossible dream"
- Needs
- Accomplishments

- Achievements
- Wants
- Values
- Interests
- Personality traits
- Temperaments
- Transferable skills and special knowledge.

"Dreams"

From early childhood, people have thoughts about what they would like to be and to do. These wishes are expressed through fantasies in play, reading selected literature, and viewing dramas and the graphic arts. Few dreams ever come to fruition, however, because realities such as time, money, talent, and motivation blunt these great ambitions. The first and most exciting task that candidates are expected to perform in their self-assessment phase is to write their "almost impossible dream." The counselor must ask them to put aside reality factors such as money and family constraints, ignore talent requisites, and just let their dreams soar.

There are two ways to get into these daydreams. One is to ask the candidate to finish the sentence, "My almost impossible dream is . . . ." The second method is to ask: "If you had your choice of all things in the world to do (present realities notwithstanding), what would you do?" How counselors get into this activity is a matter of personal style, but the goal is the same. The basic assumption is that this activity uncovers significant wishes and values long buried in the process of maturing.

These provocative questions about daydreams intrigue most candidates and send them back into childhood and youth when their dreams of future careers were developing. Candidates are encouraged to expand on the dream—to see themselves acting out their fantasies in real life, and to resist the "yes, but . . ."s of reality. They are informed that there are several points in the process where the dream is checked against reality data. Examples of vocational aspects of almost impossible dreams are "Yes, I really wanted to be a vice-president of sales." "I've always thought about being a minister." "I want to work with elderly people." "I want to be a bank manager some day."

Often the candidate dreams in more general terms, not directly related to jobs. One example is the bank executive who said, "I've always wanted to charter a sailboat in Tahiti." In this instance the candidate's dream moved from sailing lessons, to fantasies of running a sailboat outfitting service in Tahiti. He finally settled on developing a marina in the United States. His Tahiti dream steered him to boats, then to marinas, and finally to land development. The counselor helped him to combine his managerial talent with his dream.

Fantasy activities, therefore, are used to expand the candidates' awareness of job possibilities way beyond conventional, highly visible, and low-risk jobs. To help candidates overcome their resistance to following their dreams, counselors can, after they gain more information on the candidate's skills, values, needs, and wants, ask them to write a paragraph on why they cannot carry out their almost impossible dreams. To keep candidates thinking in terms of possibilities, they are asked to tell what characteristics they have learned about themselves (skills, values, needs, wants) that would help them carry out their almost impossible dreams. About one fourth of our candidates actually carried out their dreams in this three-step process of

- Writing out their almost impossible dream of what they want to do;
- Writing later, after some self-assessment, about why they cannot carry out their dream;
- Writing about how they can use their present competencies to carry out their dreams.

These dreams are checked periodically against wants, values, traits, and skills as well as against specific job functions and objectives. Finally, after the counselor winnows them through numerous reality checks, the revised fantasies are built into résumés and job campaigns. An illustration mentioned before is the evolutionary process of charter boating in Tahiti to a marina manager in Oregon.

Another illustration of how reality factors temper a dream early in the planning process is the candidate whose dream included becoming a minister. He even went as far as applying to a seminary. His wife, however, could not see herself as a minister's spouse. After considerable discussion, both decided that she could not live with his dream, and that their marriage was more important. He backed away from his dream job and chose another on his list that would also please his wife. This incident illustrates the importance of including spouses in each step of the process, and how choices are influenced by values—in this case, the overriding value was maintaining his marriage.

Needs

While it is important to start the process on a confident, uplifting note through the "almost impossible dream" activity, candidates must be concerned with some very practical and earthy considerations. Therefore, an assessment of future economic status and immediate needs for money is usually undertaken at this point. Provision must be made for survival needs during the six months or longer until the best possible job is found. Most new positions are found within four to six months. Generally, the higher the aspiration for executive jobs, the longer the search process takes. Top level executives, furthermore, like to wait for that right job that will give them power or for personal reasons.

Usually those seeking lower-level managerial positions have fewer resources to fall back upon during the lengthy job search and so are much more eager to be placed. In any case, the candidate must have the resources to live comfortably during the four to six months before placement, and to avoid panic on the campaign trail. Even though this topic of financial resources is a private matter, the counselor must become involved so that planning can be realistic if severance pay does not completely cover the job-search period.

Candidates should be urged to view this search as the biggest job they have ever had and to follow the same disciplined routines they did when they were employed. For example, they should be encouraged to get up at the usual hour and get to work on the process as if they were going to a regular job. Health habits need to be rigorously maintained. Adequate sleep cycles and exercise are important for the vitality required to stay at the task and keep tensions under control. Diet and eating habits need special scrutiny since stress and anxious, depressed feelings lead to dietary imbalances which, in turn, add to the stress.

Mood management is as important for dealing with the swings of overenthusiasm and depression, as stress management is important for dealing with tensions. Candidates need to pay particular attention to alcohol consumption since any tendency to alcohol abuse will be increased during this traumatic transition. If the outplacement counselor does not have the skills to counsel the candidates on these emotional matters, they should be referred to specialists. It is important to maintain optimum functioning during this transition period so that candidates in job interviews will present themselves at their best.

Later in the assessment process, candidates should examine needs and values to become more aware of their motivation patterns. Needs have survival values and some psychologists, such as Maslow,[1] have organized them into a hierarchical order of importance to survival. He lists physical needs as primary, followed by security, social, self-esteem, and self-actualization needs. Self-actualization means the need to realize growth potentials. Humberger[2] added psychic coping needs midway in the hierarchy and a noological need at the top of the list. Psychic coping needs pertain to candidates' needs for coping with inner pressures, and noological needs refer to the need for meaning in a person's life. People must use their intuitive capacities to transcend their physical and mental life.

They need to respond to conscience and to their unique potentialities. They need to fill that existential vacuum represented by the meaningless life. Thus, needs fall into the following hierarchy of demand, as suggested by Humberger:

- Physiological needs
- Safety
- Self-esteem
- Psychic coping
- Affection
- Social interaction
- Meaning.

The fact that needs also demand fulfillment makes this topic important to career planning. The right job fulfills most of these needs.

Accomplishments and Achievements

Positive reference letter.   Early in the assessment phase, candidates are asked, as part of their self-assessment, to draft a positive reference letter to be signed by their former employers. This letter serves two purposes: To learn what previous supervisors feel about candidates' work achievements and traits, and to provide a reference document later in the job campaign.

Corporations are reluctant to write anything very specific about employees they have fired, largely because of potential legal liabilities. It is important, however, to get a letter as soon as possible before memories fade or supervising personnel leave. The counselor asks candidates to write letters as if their former supervisors were writing them. This activity gives the candidates a chance to validate their own integrity and confirm their skills as they open their thoughts to their strengths and limitations. To help the counselor advise candidates on drafting their letters, a suggested format is included in Figure 3. Candidates then take the letters to their former supervisors and ask them to sign or to change parts of the letters to be more accurate. The signed letters are returned to the candidates.

Reference letters offer a solid base for counseling. One candidate, a vice-president, wrote a letter that he thought the president would sign— stating, among other things, that the candidate was "competent" and "cooperative." When the letter was presented to the president, he removed these two words, which infuriated the candidate. When the outplacement

---

To whom it may concern:

    I have known   for   years.   has

worked under my supervision for   years. In this position,

has performed the duties of

                  has always been a cooperative, team-oriented person.

    is knowledgeable in the field of

        is especially capable in

  Sometimes   has a tendency to

  We regret that we have had a major curtailment that requires our mutual

separation. I would be ready to take any calls for further reference in

support of

                                      Sincerely,

FIGURE 3   Sample letter of reference

counselor asked the president if it were true that the candidate was not competent and cooperative, he replied, "He certainly was not. Otherwise we wouldn't have fired him. He couldn't do the job and he couldn't get along with his peers." The counseling task, then, was to help the candidate become more keenly aware of the discrepancies between his perceptions and those of his former peers, his communication problems, and how to receive negative feedback. While this kind of counseling for personal change was not easy, the initial breakthrough came when he was writing the reference letter.

    Life history.   Early in the assessment phase the candidate is asked to complete an activity history covering work, education, leisure, military service, and community involvement. In addition to providing the counselor and candidate with a panoramic view of the candidate's life, it provides the basic data for summarizing accomplishments and achievements. Numerous examples of life history forms exist, but one that we have found most useful was developed by Robert Jameson.[3] This form emphasizes present interests and activities as well as work and educational history.

The candidate abstracts from the history form a list of accomplishments and achievements in four areas—educational, vocational, community, and recreational. For example, educational accomplishments are listed in five-year age groups from childhood through the present. Achievements then are starred. In this context, accomplishments are defined as those tasks one has completed, while achievements are defined as those tasks liked and accomplished with exemplary results. Achievements lead one to say, "I like what I did and I did it extremely well." Achievements imply development of skills. For example, becoming a Boy Scout is an accomplishment, while becoming an Eagle Scout is an achievement. A candidate says, "I started a business when I was forty [an accomplishment], and I sold it at a profit at age fifty [an achievement]." To say "I am a machinist" is an accomplishment, but to indicate that "Everyone in the shop calls upon me to do their precision work" is an achievement.

The primary purpose of this listing activity is to identify demonstrated skills through achievements. Interests are also inferred from this lifetime record of achievements since they usually represent activities that were enjoyed. These inferred skills and motives are checked against other assessments of abilities and interests. Finally, in the next phase of outplacement counseling, the composite of skills, needs, values, and wants is translated into job functions and job titles.

To prepare for the next step of developing job targets, five major achievements are selected. These five achievements are then checked against a list of job requirements such as John Holland's six categories of job themes in "The Self-Directed Search,"[4] or Richard Bolles' categories in "The Quick Job-Hunting Map."[5] Patterns are noted and are checked further with interest and value inventories to be described in the next sections.

Wants

Wants are more specific than the "almost impossible dream" described earlier. These are tangible outcomes the candidates really want from a job. Examples are travel, new friends, higher salary, independence, and chances for personal growth. Candidates are asked to list their wants, which become the specifications list for the ideal job. Many of these wants are also classified as values, such as independence or wealth. The major purpose of this analysis of wants, needs, values, and interests is to get an accurate picture of the candidates' motivations—that driving force that accounts for a large part of job success.

Values

Values are ideas we hold dear, such as personal freedom and independence. They are central meanings shared by a group of people, such as loyalty and service. Families have been the traditional transmitting institutions for basic values; later, adults learn values that cluster around work, social relationships, and life struggles. Basic values affect a person's self-esteem since all life experiences are filtered through that person's value system. When the values of other members of a person's group vary drastically with his or her own values, self-esteem may be jeopardized. Such value conflicts among members of a social group lead to a loss of personal identity as well as worth. Different jobs and work settings have different values associated with them, and the counselor's task is to find the best fit between the job's value requirements and the candidate's personal values. For example, some employees prefer easy work and consistent supervision; whereas others value pay, influence, security, or friendly working relationships.

Assessing Values

Values come in various combinations, of course, but they are presented here to emphasize the wide range of individual differences in work values. These values determine why people work and whether they will be happy and successful on their jobs. The problem is that the precise value weightings that predict success on a given job are unknown. The counselor must do the best he or she can to infer relationships between assessed values and job requirements.

A number of illustrative instruments that measure values are available. They must be used with caution, however, so a candidate is not classified too narrowly. A sufficient number of comparative questions are asked about what people think is important so the counselor will get a picture of their dominant values. The Rokeach Value Survey, for example, forces choices among eighteen value statements. The answers given in value inventories offer many clues for counseling. For example, to note discrepancies, values important to the candidate are compared with achievements.

Interests

Interests are preferences for specific activities—both career and non-career related. Interest inventories compare the candidate's interests to the interest patterns of a large group of people who were satisfied and successful on their jobs. The Strong-Campbell Interest Inventory[6] has a long developmental history of assessing adult interests and is well known in industrial personnel offices and career planning services. It must be machine scored. Results are reported for 162 occupational scales, twenty-three basic interest scores, and six Holland theme scores based on John Holland's theory of six occupational personalities.

The Johansson Career Assessment Inventory (CAI)[7] is an interest measure patterned after the Strong-Campbell measure. It was developed for adults seeking immediate career entry in middle-level business and technical careers, especially those usually sought after secondary or two-year college work. The CAI requires machine scoring from specially designed computer centers.

Traits

Personality traits and patterns are very important to job success, particularly those pertaining to human relations. The problem with assessment and prediction is that research results have not been very promising in relating personality trait measures to success on particular jobs. Consequently, personality inventories are used mainly to uncover topics and problems that are unlikely to hinder job adjustment. Counselors have their own favorites among the many personality inventories on the market. One that we have used consistently is the *Sixteen Personality Factor Questionnaire.*[8] This inventory is machine scored and emphasizes normal personality characteristics. The 16 PF assesses levels of assertiveness, emotional maturity, shrewdness, self-sufficiency, tension, and eleven other primary traits. The instrument has been used widely in business and industry for selection and placement, as well as for promotion decisions and counseling, since it attempts to predict important job-related criteria.

Temperaments

Temperament is a broad personality disposition closely related to interests. Assessment in this area is useful for candidates since it gives them data on dominant tendencies such as movement away from or toward people. Such measures tend to confirm candidates' own judgments, although occasionally candidates are surprised by the results.

An illustrative inventory useful in the early stages of counseling is the Meyers-Briggs Type Indicator.[9] This measure of disposition and interest is based on Carl Jung's typology of personalities. Results are reported on four bipolar scales—introversion–extroversion, sensing–intuition, thinking–feeling, and judging–perceptive. This inventory holds candidate interest and its content is nonthreatening. While space does not permit mention of the growing body of research on the MBTI, it is useful in career counseling and executive development for indicating broad directions and tendencies. For example, a candidate may have been dreaming of going into sales promotion work; yet his MBTI self-assessment indicates leanings to high introversion. This cues a topic for counseling about whether the candidate's temperament matches job requirements and if other assessment data are sufficiently close to infer satisfaction.

The MBTI is helpful in counseling on communication patterns with spouses. For example, the candidate and spouse take the inventories at the same time and the counselor helps them to discuss comparative profiles.

Abilities (Skills)

Ability is inferred from work and educational history, as indicated in the earlier discussion of achievements. Direct psychometric assessment of abilities is not useful with mature adults unless it is to predict the outcome of a highly specific kind of training, such as undergraduate engineering. Therefore, we need to depend on a careful analysis of the candidate's achievement record for clues about transferable skills. For job targets in which the candidate has no specific achievement record, we need to depend on interest and value predictors of satisfaction that apply to numerous jobs.

Richard Bolles[10] has developed an inventory of transferable skills, cited earlier, that allows candidates to extract from their life experiences the relevant skills utilized in that experience. The hundreds of skills are classified as manual, outdoor, detail, and so on. If one had run a successful party, for example, skills in designing, coordinating, recruiting, and organizing were demonstrated. The personal experiences are listed at the top and relevant skills listed in the inventory are checked so that patterns immediately become apparent. Krannich and Banis,[11] in their study, found that most adults possess between 600 and 800 transferable skills that can be utilized in jobs in business, industry, and government.

General Batteries

Two principles must be kept in the foreground during this assessment phase. The first is to realize that the tasks involve self-assessment and, consequently, that the data come from the candidates' own choices. There is no mystery about this process or profound revelations of "who I am" and "what I am like." The second counseling principle is to keep the career-planning goal clearly in mind. There is a temptation to wander on tangents and interesting byways of self-exploration that may have little to do with finding that next job.

An instrument that applies both of the principles just mentioned is John Holland's *Self-Directed Search,*[12] cited earlier. This is a sixteen-page booklet that leads candidates into thoughtful evaluations of their abilities, interests, traits, and values. This evaluation stimulates an active exploration of jobs in Holland's companion booklet, *Occupation Finder.*[13] The candidates complete, score, and interpret the results themselves. The results are compiled into six categories: realistic, investigative, artistic, enterprising, social, and conventional. These categories, from Holland's theory of vocations, are used as descriptive labels throughout the outplacement counseling process. So, candidates and counselors should become thoroughly familiar with the work clusters illustrated as follows:

- Realistic: Prefers activities involving mechanical skill, physical strength, outdoor tasks, often with plants and animals.
- Investigative: Prefers activities involving thinking, research, and problem solving. Curious, observant, and prefers working with ideas more than people.
- Artistic: Values self-expression and creativity. Tends to be emotional, imaginative, and innovative. Enjoys unstructured situations.
- Enterprising: Likes to persuade others and usually is skilled in public speaking. Likes to initiate, organize, lead, and negotiate.
- Social: Enjoys working with others in teaching and helping. Exhibits effective communication and listening.
- Conventional: Prefers structure and order. Work often involves good memory and close attention to details and figures.

The research base for Holland's work is cited in *Making Vocational Choices: A Theory of Careers.*[14]

SUMMARIZING AND INTEGRATING ASSESSMENT RESULTS

The first task facing candidates is to absorb the details of the assessment. Candidates should be given copies of profiles so they can study results at their leisure. The counselor has interpreted all the data, pointing out patterns, consistencies, and discrepancies, and has checked continually for feedback from the candidates to determine their levels of understanding of results.

The second task is to condense results and emphasize patterns. The

---

Skills--Chronology of Achievements (and in Holland Categories)

_____   _____
_____   _____
_____   _____

Traits Summary (and in Holland Categories)

_____   _____
_____   _____
_____   _____

Interests (Highest occupational scales and Holland categories)

_____   _____
_____   _____
_____   _____

Self-Directed Search Summary of Holland Categories Wants (5 top desires)

_____   _____
_____   _____
_____   _____

My Almost Impossible Dream (key components)

_____   _____
_____   _____
_____   _____

Needs: Satisfied   Deficient

_____   _____
_____   _____
_____   _____

Values (Main Clusters)
         Values not Achieved   Achievements not Valued

_____   _____
_____   _____
_____   _____

FIGURE 4   Assessment summary sheet

counselor prepares a summary sheet that lists the principal findings of the assessment efforts, as illustrated in Figure 4. This completed summary is given to the candidates for their records and a copy is retained by the counselor for later reference during job targeting and for accountability reports.

To facilitate understanding of assessment data, candidates should be asked to write a few paragraphs about their understanding of the results and about how the results might be used in their personal growth and job search. Candidates write about "The personal growth I need in order to use my skills and values and attain my needs and wants." For example, one candidate—finding that he was very cautious and conservative in almost all domains—decided that one of his directions for growth was to take more risks and to reach out to people more often.

When the assessment steps just described are completed satisfactorily, the candidate is ready to develop job targeting and résumé writing.

SUMMARY

Assessment methods in outplacement counseling include observation and testing of values, wants, interests, skills, traits, accomplishments, and achievements. These data form the bases for choices of job targets. An important byproduct from assessment of strengths and achievements is the positive effect on the candidate's self-esteem. Assessment batteries should be tailored to the needs of each candidate and should be administered and interpreted under strict professional guidelines.

NOTES

[1]Abraham Maslow, *Motivation and Personality,* 2nd ed. (New York: Harper and Row, 1970). An application of Maslow's need hierarchy to counseling may be found in L. M. Brammer, *The Helping Relationship: Process and Skills,* 2nd ed. (Englewood Cliffs, N.J.: Prentice-Hall, 1979).

[2]Frank Humberger expanded Maslow's list. An unpublished list with illustrations may be obtained from Dr. Frank Humberger, Executive Services Associates, Lincoln Center, 244, Bellevue, WA 98004.

[3]Robert Jameson, *The Professional Job Changing System* (Parsippany, N.J.: Performance Dynamics, 1977).

[4]John Holland, *The Self-Directed Search: A Professional Manual,* is distributed by Psychological Assessment Resources, Box 98, Odessa, FL 33556.

[5]Richard N. Bolles, *The Quick Job-Hunting Map* (Berkeley, CA: Ten Speed Press, 1979). Bolles's system is explained in *What Color Is Your Parachute?* (Berkeley, CA: Ten Speed Press, 1981).

[6]*Strong-Campbell Interest Inventory.* Palo Alto: Consulting Psychologist Press, 557 College Avenue, 94306.

[7]C. B. Johansson, *Manual for the Career Assessment Inventory* (Minneapolis: National Computer Systems, 1976).

[8]Raymond Cattell, *Sixteen Personality Factor Questionnaire* (16PF) is distributed by Psychological Assessment Resources, PO Box 98, Odessa, FL 33556. Also useful is Raymond Cattell and others, *The 16 PF Handbook, 1970* from the same distributor.

[9]Isabell Meyers and Catherine Briggs, *The Meyers-Briggs Type Indicator,*

is distributed by Psychological Assessment Resources, Box 98, Odessa, FL 33556.

[10]Bolles, *Quick Job-Hunting Map.*

[11]R. L. Krannich and W. J. Banis, *High Impact Résumés and Letters* (New York: Progressive Concepts, 1982).

[12]Holland, *Self-Directed Search.*

[13]Holland, *Occupation Finder,* a list of representative occupations in six work clusters to use with Holland's *Self-Directed Search,* Psychological Assessment Resources, Box 98, Odessa, FL 33556.

[14]J. L. Holland, *Making Vocational Choices: A Theory of Careers* (Englewood Cliffs, N.J.: Prentice-Hall, 1983).

5

Self-Directed Job Targeting

The goal of job targeting in Stage 7 is the preparation of a list of three jobs that would appeal to the candidate and would match his or her qualifications. The match would be so precise that job résumés would convince prospective employers that he or she is the preferred candidate. Self-marketing is most effective when candidates, aware of who they are, decide what specific jobs best fit their assessed skills, needs, wants, and values. Candidates also must be clear about their preferred work arena or job setting. To help candidates choose work arenas and job settings much information about the job market is needed. The list of reading resources at the end of this chapter will be valuable in this search for suitable arenas and job objectives.

STEPS IN JOB TARGETING

- Review skills from assessment summary
- Review the "almost impossible dream" and its analysis
- Choose five top priority skills from the master list
- Match the five skills to specific job functions
- Choose appropriate job arenas
- Write three to five job objectives
- Write three to five job résumés to match the job objectives

Matching Skills
to Functions

Reviewing skills and comparing them to the "almost impossible dream" prepare the candidates for prioritizing their skills. Part of this analysis is to do a force-field study of the dream, by listing barriers against, and strengths supporting it. An optimum decision often emerges.

The top five skills are selected and matched with job functions. These functions are found in directories and dictionaries of job titles. The *Dictionary of Occupational Titles*[1] (DOT) is the principal source. Other examples, such as *The Occupational Outlook Handbook*[2] and *Guide for Occupational Exploration*,[3] supplement the DOT. These resources help candidates determine which specific job titles best fit their skills. Usually this search will produce thirty-five to fifty different job functions. The candidate must consider the domain or arenas of possible work, which helps to reduce the final list of possible job objectives to five.

When candidates have found their best fit in one or more of Holland's six work clusters, they can look up specific occupations in the *Dictionary of Holland Occupational Codes*.[4] This is a comprehensive cross-indexed list of 12,000 DOT occupations keyed to Holland's six occupational codes.

Choosing Job Arenas

A job arena can be a *discipline,* such as sociology or theology; it can be an *industry,* such as steel or electronics; it can be a *service,* such as banking or counseling; it can include *environments,* such as participative management, small business, or a location such as the southwestern states.

Candidates should think over their five preferred job targets in terms of attractive arenas. Market information about the future of that arena should be considered. For example, is it likely to become obsolete? This information can be obtained from libraries stocking standard registers of business, educational, or governmental organizations and indexes of regular publications, such as *The Wall Street Journal* and *Business Week.* This task may involve several hours of research, but it is essential for a solid base from which the candidates will choose their final job targets.

Job arenas, whether disciplines and industries or geographic location, differ in the amounts of per capita income. For example, *U.S. News & World Report*[5] quoted a U.S. Commerce Department report on per capita incomes in major U.S. cities for 1980. These incomes varied from $10,623 in a Southern and a Northwestern city, to $14,266 in Anchorage, Alaska. Salaries for middle-level managers rose from 1981 to 1982, according to a survey of the Administrative Management Society.[6] Plant, sales, and personnel managers earned an average base salary of $27,861 in 1982, a 7.6 percent increase over 1981. The highest rate of increase was west of the Rocky Mountains. Candidates must, at this point, take another look at their lists of needs, wants, and values to help them choose appropriate arenas.

Writing Job Objectives

When the tasks outlined in the previous section are completed to their satisfaction, candidates are ready to make the final commitment to job objectives. These objectives are written as follows:

I want to obtain a job as (job function):_____

preferably in the field of (job arena):_____

in an environment of (arena and wants):_____
at a salary of:_____and to start by:_____

Each of the five objectives is written in this general format. When writing them, certain feelings and ideas will emerge that affirm or cast doubt on the objective. Examples are "I would really like to do that kind of work, but my family needs more income than this job would afford," "I would like to work for that company, but my research shows me that they do not give enough support to engineers such as myself," "I need a structured environment such as that engineering company, but I don't get the impression from my research so far that I could be happy with the boss," "I would like to be a minister since it is of such high value to me, but my wife does not want to participate in this work, and I would feel at a loss without her."

After the soul searching that follows writing job objectives, the list of five is often narrowed to three. Before they give in to the temptation to move immediately to writing résumés, candidates should be encouraged to make a final check of these job objectives against their needs, wants, values, personal strengths, and limitations, prior to thinking of them as final. This is done through checking data already gathered and by simulating performance in that job and setting. Counselors attempt to simulate the future job performance of the candidate, and identify the obstacles (personal or job) that might interfere. Visualization of performance is a powerful tool for candidates to test possibilities and to clarify how they would perform in particular jobs.

During this analysis of their strengths and limitations, candidates should ask themselves, "What can I do to enhance my strengths and minimize or remove my shortcomings or change them into strengths?" We will now consider examples of how analyses of personal strengths and weaknesses are related to job objectives.

George T. had many strengths related to his work. He was very proficient in the technicalities of finance, an efficient planner, and reasonably effective in his interpersonal relationships. When he was promoted to a new job, however, within six months his attention to it diminished, resulting in his dismissal. He was preoccupied by his personal life, which limited his productivity. Counseling straightened out his personal life before he contracted for another position.

Mary S., terminated from a production supervisor position, expressed suspicion and caution about applying for a new position in supervision because "they'll get me no matter where I apply. I'm in a male-dominated field and they are out to clean women out of their ranks." Since Mary had been in this position for seven years, and in a previous supervisory position for six years, this claim was explored with a female counselor. Together, they were able to perceive the realities of the job setting more accurately, and to separate the realities of the job situation from Mary's biases. Then Mary tested herself with two male counselors who put her through some stress-interviewing to prepare her for reentry into the job market. Mary now works in a personnel department with a 75 percent female work force. She is pleased with the opportunity to test herself in another environment.

Willard J. claims he had no idea why he was fired, although his superiors told the outplacement counselor that his unit was in shambles because of his stubborn, autocratic, and arrogant traits. He was capable technically, but his abrasiveness was a career liability. He went to work on this problem in counseling prior to beginning his job campaign.

Don B. was an affable and capable retired Navy officer who went into business. He was released for antagonizing employees with his autocratic demands. He could not understand why his orders to business associates were not carried out. His lack of awareness of the methods of participative management and the carryover of his military approaches were distinct shortcomings that he had to correct before he could be a successful business manager.

Bob J. had not accepted the accusations of his former employees that he was abrasive, especially toward women. After some counseling he perceived more clearly his shortcomings in relationships with people and attempted to change them during his job campaign.

These examples point out, first, that the candidates needed to become more aware of their shortcomings and to make changes before completing their job campaigns. Failures on the job often have little to do with technical skills. Second, it is important to note that the task of changing was up to the candidates. The counselor helped the candidates to become aware that they could capitalize on their strengths and not be sabotaged by their limitations, but the candidates themselves had to act on that awareness.

Counselors' styles differ in bringing this awareness to candidates. Some present the evidence directly in a confrontive manner. Others use more indirect methods, such as Socratic questioning, to get them to arrive at this clearer awareness of themselves. For example, the counselor might ask, "How is that trait going to help or hinder you in your job campaign?" In any case, it is important to clear up potential liabilities before moving to the final phase in preparation for self-marketing: Writing the job résumé and training for the job interview.

WRITING RÉSUMÉS

Why Résumés?

Constructing résumés helps candidates to acquire self-knowledge and to improve their self-esteem in preparation for interviews. Résumés promote the candidates' self-confidence when the candidates see their achievements, strengths, and outstanding performances concisely packaged. An effective résumé conveys the impression that the candidate can do a good job for an employer.

Candidates must realize that it is the interview, not the résumé, that gets the job! It informs the interviewer about why the person is seeking the job and it offers a brief recitation of documented skills. It can also serve to legitimate the candidate and give the interviewer leads for further questions.

Lathrop[7] advises using a qualifications brief (to be described later), which emphasizes abilities and presents a persuasive case for the candidate. He claims that most résumés are too long and are discarded because they do not emphasize what the candidate can do. Such a brief should focus on the needs of the employer instead of the usual emphasis on the applicant's needs.

Each résumé is tailored to a specific job, since employers like to see résumés closely related to the job being filled. Therefore, candidates should construct three résumés to match each of their three top job targets. These résumés are the final result of the candidates' research on themselves and their target jobs. In the superior résumé, these specific qualifications should, as W. Cohen,[8] an executive search expert, expressed it, be stated concisely and concretely.

Résumés are the candidate's advance representatives to potential employers. To make a favorable impression, plain, white, letter-sized paper and ordinary type styles should be used. Content and style should reflect the unique qualities of the candidate, but all statements should be brief and to the point. Above all, the résumé should *not appear to be commercially prepared*. Candidates should be advised to place themselves in the position of readers by asking: "Is it relevant? Is it clear? Is it factual? Is it brief? Is it documented?" Items should be indented for emphasis. In general, the résumé should be impressive on its own merits without appearing ostentatious or containing misleading data.

Résumés are sometimes confused with vitae, which are longer and more general. Professional and technical candidates might be encouraged to prepare this companion document, which lists their bibliographies, honors, travels, and consultancies. Vitae are used commonly in academic and governmental employment situations, but they are not substitutes for the one- or two-page résumé.

The Effective Résumé

An effective résumé should include

- Identifying information (name, address, and telephone number)
- Employment objective
- Achievements and, or, qualifications
- Experience
- Education and training
- Personal (additional qualifications and offer of references).

Employment objective.   This is a concise statement of the job objective. Examples are "entry level position in public relations," "a management position in the engineering design/control systems field," "project manager in marketing." Usually, the objective is limited to one or two sentences and can include the desired arena, such as "a small corporation with a progressive management."

Qualification or achievement summaries.   Summaries are used to focus the reader on the highlights of the candidate's achievements and special qualifications that fit the proposed job objective. This usually is a bulleted list of four to six items stressing specific data. Particular emphasis should be given to activities that reduced costs and increased profits. All data must be documented to protect the credibility of the applicant.

Professional experiences.   The résumé should include the dates and locations of experiences that document the candidate's skills. A sentence accurately describing the levels of responsibility should follow that documentation. Inaccuracies cast doubt on the veracity and judgment of the candidate. Usually only the last 15–20 years of activities are cited. If interviewers want to know more about those early job years, they will ask.

Educational background.   Achievements, special competencies, and updating of skills should be emphasized. Dates and locations of the training should be documented accurately. Stories float around academic circles about the large number of people who carelessly cite academic achievement data or deceptively mention degrees they never earned. These data are verified easily, and employers may do so. If certain qualifications such as an MBA degree or a doctorate are required, this information should be listed near the beginning of the résumé; otherwise, educational and personal material are placed at the end of the résumé.

Personal data.   Personal data are matters of taste and judgment. Usually included are health and family data; hobbies or writing interests are rarely mentioned in current résumés. Stating information about age, marital status, and race feeds prejudicial stereotypes and so is best left to the interviewer to observe or discover. If mentioned, that information should convey the idea of a balanced life.

Chronological or Functional Format?

There are two basic formats for résumés, although combinations are used frequently. Recently added is the "Qual Brief" résumé listing the job objective and a summary of key abilities and achievements.

The chronological format.   The chronological format is a listing of items by dates of occurrence.

- Employment objective
- Background summary (past job functions that support the employment objective)

- Work experience (listed chronologically for the past 15–20 years with dates of employment, names and addresses of employers, titles held, brief description of responsibilities, and significant achievements)
- Education and training (usually reverse chronology, listing most recent experiences first)
- Personal items (memberships, publications).

One chronological type is illustrated in Figure 5. Financial advisers, for example, prefer the chronological format to help interviewers check credibility with former colleagues and clients.

[Name]
[Address]
[Telephone]

OBJECTIVE

A management position that will give me the opportunity to apply my experience and skills in the Engineering Design/Control Systems field.

PROFESSIONAL EXPERIENCE

1977-   [company name] Corporate Engineering Department--Manager,
Present   Electrical and Control Systems.

           Responsible for electrical, process control, human factors, and design safety for capital projects and support to operating mills.

           · Reorganized and staffed the process control function.
           · Supervised a management team responsible for 43 direct profes-
           · sionals and up to 200 outside consultant resources.
           · Integrated electrical and process control disciplines for opti-
             mum coordination of design effort.
           · Implemented use of Computer-Aided-Design technology for design
             and construction documents.
           · Initiated and monitored development of process control training
             programs for mill operators and maintenance personnel.
           · Interacted with management in mills, businesses, research, and
             informations systems.
           · Accountable for annual capital expenditures up to $60,000,000
             per year.

1976-   [company name]--General Superintendent, Manufacturing
1977
           Responsible for powerhouse and chemical plant operations in large
           multi-product chemical plant as a career development assignment.

           · Supervised 16 salaried and 120 hourly employees.
           · Participated in grievance process and contract negotiations.
           · Responded to emergencies.
           · Conducted safety programs.
           · Accountable for safety, product quality, and production and an
             annual budget of approximately $50,000,000 per year.

FIGURE 5   Example of chronological résumé

```
1965-    [company name]
1976
         Corporate Engineering Department--Manager, Engineering.
         Electrical and Instrument design section.  1969-1976.

         Responsible for electrical and instrumentation design for chemical
         and petrochemical plants.

         . Supervised 20 direct professionals and consultants performing
           design in-house and outside.

1957-    Inorganic Chemicals Division--Instruction Supervisor, 1963-1965.
1965
         Responsible for new technological projects and instrumentation
         design for new and existing plants.

         . Specified and installed first direct digital control computer.
         . Supervised 6 professionals handling instrumentation studies and
           design.

         Inorganic Chemicals Division--Instrument Engineer, 1957-1963.

         Responsible for instrumentation projects and technical support in new
         and existing plants.

         . Designed and started up instrumentation systems for new plants.
         . Performed special studies and implemented sophisticated systems
           to solve operating problems.

1951-    [company name]
1957
         Instrument engineer and supervisor responsible for plans projects
         and maintenance of instrumentation for phenol, formalin, and resin
         compounding plants.

EDUCATION

Case Institute of Technology BSChE--1949
Case Institute of Technology, Attended Systems Engineering Graduate School,
   1959-1960.

PROFESSIONAL

Instrument Society of America, Senior Member
   National Chairman--Education Committee
   General Chairman--1973 Joint Conference in St. Louis
   Section Offices--President, Vice-President, Secretary, Program Chairman
```

FIGURE 5   (Continued)

Functional résumés.   A functional résumé does not list items by dates, but rather focuses on skills represented by achievements and/or functions. Functional résumés have four sections:

- Qualifications or background summary,
- Achievements listed as effective functions or proven skills,
- Work experiences and education,
- Optional personal items (association memberships, honors).

Figure 6 includes a functional résumé of the same candidate cited in Figure 5, allowing comparisons to be made on the basic types. Figure

[Name]
[Address]
[Telephone]

CAREER OBJECTIVES

A management position that will give me the opportunity to apply my
experience and skills in the Engineering Design/Control Systems field

SELECTED ACHIEVEMENTS

Management

- MANAGED organizations consisting of 30 to 50 professionals engaged
  in process control and electrical engineering.
- REORGANIZED and STAFFED the process control function in a corporate engineering department.
- DIRECTED internal personnel and up to 200 external consultant
  resources in all aspects of the process control and electrical
  portions of capital projects.
- MANAGED the expenditure of up to $60,000,000 per year for
  installed systems.
- MANAGED the operation of a multi-product chemical plant and utilities system having an annual operating budget of $50,000,000 per year.
- MANAGED the development of a corporate process control training
  school which has been in operation for 12 years. Over 200 new
  graduate engineers have attended this school.
- MANAGED the development of computer-aided design techniques for
  construction documents. This system resulted in production of
  electrical drawings at less than one-half the cost of manual methods.

Engineering and Technology

- SPECIFIED the first full-scale direct digital computer control
  system in the chemical industry and SUPERVISED its installation
  and successful start-up.
- PLANNED AND IMPLEMENTED process control systems for a variety of
  batch and continuous chemical plants.
- DESIGNED AND STARTED UP special control systems to solve difficult
  problems in operating plants.
- PROMOTED and UTILIZED the latest state-of-the-art technology in
  measurement and control. Examples are:
- Distributed control systems
- Programmable controllers
- Electronic analog controllers
- Microprocessor-based systems
- Hierarchical process control computer systems

RESUME DATA

Professional

    Instrument Society of America--Senior Member
       National Chairman--Education Committee
       General Chairman--1973 Joint Conference in St. Louis
       Section Offices--President, Vice-President, Secretary, Program Chairman
    TAPPI--Member

Publications

"University Education and the Instrument Engineer in the Chemical
Industry," ISA Conference Proceedings, 1965.

"The Computer--Operator Interface," Control Engineering, 1966.

"Control Systems for Prevention of Hazardous Material Spills in Process
Plants," Material Conference on Hazardous Material Spills, 1971.

FIGURE 6   Example of functional résumé

```
Education

   Case Institute of Technology BSChE--1949.
   Case Institute of Technology--Attended Systems Engineering Graduate
      School, 1959-1960.

Career Overview

   1977-Present. Weyerhaeuser Company, Tacoma, Washington
   Corporate Engineering--Manager, Electrical and Control Systems Design.

   1976-1977. Monsanto Company, St. Louis, Missouri
   John F. Queeny Plant--General Superintendent, Manufacturing.

   1965-1976. Monsanto Company, St. Louis, Missouri
   Corporate Engineering--Manager, Engineering Electrical and Instrument
   Design Section. 1967-1976--Engineering Supervisor, Instrument design.
```

FIGURE 6   (Continued)

7 is a "Qual Brief" of the same candidate. Figures 8 and 9 contain additional examples of functional résumés. Figure 8 illustrates achievements listed as past positions, and Figure 9 illustrates achievements listed as skills. In Figure 6 it may also be noted how the "Background Summary" focuses the reader on a brief look at past responsibilities. Selected achievements on functional résumés are expressed in specific numbers and the employment history is brief. Candidates with sporadic work records, such as homemakers who have moved in and out of the job market, should select the functional format to focus on their marketable skills.

Combination résumés. A combination résumé shows experience arranged chronologically, but stresses the candidate's skills. Ordinarily, education is not listed first, but if the educational qualifications for the position are high or if there are certain requirements such as a masters degree or doctorate, they should be listed first.

PRINCIPLES OF CONSTRUCTING AND DISTRIBUTING RÉSUMÉS

The focus of this chapter has been the presentation of positive guidelines for effective résumés.

- Résumés are written, in part, to give confidence to candidates in interviews.

[Name]
[Address]
[Telephone]

OBJECTIVE

A management position that will give me the opportunity to apply my
experience and skills in the Engineering Design/Control Systems field.

QUALIFICATIONS

Five years with a major forest products company as upper-level Corporate
Engineering manager responsible for both electrical and process control design.

- Reorganized and staffed the process control function.
- Supervised a management team responsible for 43 direct professionals
  and up to 200 external consultant resources.
- Integrated electrical, process control, and human factors functions.
- Implemented use of Computer-Aided Design technology.
- Initiated and monitored development of process control training
  programs for plant personnel.
- Interacted with operations management, research, & information systems.
- Accountable for capital expenditures of up to $40-60,000,000 per year.

Twenty years with a major chemical company in various engineering and
management positions.

- One year career development assignment as manufacturing superintendent
  responsible for utilities, waste treatment, and chemical production.
- Eleven years in corporate engineering management responsible for
  electrical and instrumentation design.

  .. Supervised 50 professionals responsible for in-house design and
     external consultant management.
  .. Managed the corporate instrument engineering training program.
  .. Developed the process control computer systems function.
  .. Developed an automated design document system.

- Eight years as instrument engineer and supervisor in a division engineering department.

  .. Supervised new process control technology projects.
  .. Planned, designed, and started up process control systems for new
     plants and modifications to others.
  .. Provided trouble-shooting support to all operating plants.

Six years with resin manufacturing company as process engineer and plant
chief instrument engineer.

- Performed process engineering for new cumene phenol plant.
- Organized and supervised instrument maintenance department.
- Designed and installed new instrumentation system as plant improvement
  projects.

FIGURE 7   Example of "qual brief" résumé

```
                            [Name]
                           [Address]
                          [Telephone]


CAREER DIRECTION:       Senior Executive position utilizing marketing and
                        analytical skills in managing organizations.


BACKGROUND SUMMARY:

Experience:             Twenty years in senior, middle, and staff positions in
                        the financial and insurance industries in administra-
                        tive managerial functions including selection,
                        training, and development of people; planning and
                        budgeting; allocation of resources; implementation of
                        policies and procedures, and establishment of finan-
                        cial controls in achieving specific goals.

Education:              B.S. Industrial Relations Personnel Administration,
                        ABC University, 1967.

Affiliations:           Board Member, Mortgage Bankers Association, United Way.


SELECTED ACHIEVEMENTS

Marketing Manager:      Increased market share in title insurance company from
                        10% to 25% and increased pre-tax profit from $40K to
                        $9.5 M per year in four years.

                        Expanded company operations from 3 counties to 25
                        counties by negotiating the purchases of existing com-
                        panies, establishing new branch and agency facilities
                        and selling branches to independent operators through-
                        out the state of Washington.

Organizational          Directed, researched, and implemented the reorganiza-
Manager, Developer:     tion of work flow for a title insurance company which
                        reduced handling of accounts directly increasing capa-
                        city and market share.

Operations Auditor:     Functioned as Chief Auditor for major insurance com-
                        pany covering U.S. and Canada.  Audited levels of
                        operating efficiency, adequacy of work flow, service
                        and accounting controls, efficient staff levels, and
                        expense controls.  Recommended multiple cost/time
                        saving procedures.


EMPLOYMENT HISTORY:     Sr. Vice President/Division Manager, Portland, Oregon,
                        1978-1982

                        Sr. Vice President Administrator, Aetna Insurance, 1977.

                        Management Trainee, Seattle, Washington, 1960-1961.

                        Shop Clerk, Seattle, Washington, 1958-1960.


PERSONAL:               Married, health excellent.


REFERENCES:             Available upon request.
```

**FIGURE 8   Example of functional résumé (achievements listed as posi-
tions held)**

- Résumés should be examined carefully for repetition, especially in detailing achievements and work experience.
- Candidates should not always include résumés with broadcast letters (described in the next chapter). Usually a Qual Brief is an appropriate substitute for a résumé. The goal is to whet an interviewer's curiosity but not give too much information.
- Mailing résumés should be avoided, even when the candidate is requested to do so in a phone call. Candidates should resist being

---

[Name]
[Address]
[Telephone]

SUMMARY OF QUALIFICATIONS

Sixteen years of experience in Comptrollership/Accounting with a large, integrated forest products firm:

Supervision: As Regional Comptroller, directed staff of 120 (11 direct) in seven operating locations, managing all aspects of regional comptrollership.

Technical/Financial: Division Accounting Management, Corporate Headquarters Accounting, Cost Accounting, Divisional General Accounting, Acquisition Accounting, SEC Reporting, Credit Supervision, Federal Price Controls.

Systems and Data Processing Administration

SELECTED ACHIEVEMENTS

Policy   Created new regional controllers organization, responsible for
Developer   all aspects of controllership of seven divisions in Washington
                and Alaska. Total regional sales of approximatley $300 million.

                Developed with regional management improved systems for inter-
                division transfer of raw materials which enhanced ability to
                evaluate individual unit performance.

                Wrote and implemented regional accounting policies controlling
                capitalization of logging roads and treatment of forestry
                overheads, which were adopted as corporate policy. Developed
                and issued several policies that controlled accounting prac-
                tices for a new partnership business.

Problem   Corrected deficiencies in financial controls and reporting for
Solver   company's largest profit division via an operational review,
Innovator   personnel reorganization, and systems modification.

                Developed improved systems for tracking cost improvement
                program results. Revised system was adopted company-wide,
                resulting in significant manpower savings.

FIGURE 9   Example of functional résumé (achievements listed as skills)

Directed the integration of three new lumber manufacturing facilities into the corporate accounting and reporting system. Additionally, directed the development of all financial systems for startup of new chemical products manufacturing facility.

Financial
Evaluator

Designed and implemented Financial Management Control System which was adopted as the operational control system for all fourteen operating divisions of the company.

Facilitated recovery of an additional $50K by developing alternative negotiating strategies in sale of company's equity in a sawmill partnership.

S & DP
Administrator

Managed the development and initial installation of Data Processing Departments in two locations. Tangible savings from on-going DP applications exceed the $1.0 million annual budget.

Created a Requirements Definition and Software Package Selection System for two major accounting systems, and prepared for installation of General Ledger System in Northwest Division.

EMPLOYMENT HISTORY [Company and inclusive dates of employment]

Regional Comptroller, Seattle, Washington	1979-1983
Assistant Comptroller, New York, New York	1977-1978
Assistant to the Comptroller, New York, New York	1974-1976
Division Comptroller, Port Angeles, Washington	1966-1973
Assistant Division Comptroller, Hoquiam, Washington	1963-1965
Accountant, Hoquiam, Washington	1957-1962

EDUCATION

AB, Whitman College, Walla Walla, Washington, 1963.

Miscellaneous courses in Timber Taxation, Computer Security, Management Skills, etc.

PERSONAL

Health excellent, age 44, married, two children at home.

REFERENCES

Available upon request.

FIGURE 9   (Continued)

interviewed by phone, which may kill an opportunity for a personal interview.

- It is not wise for the candidate to volunteer, when phoning for appointments, that he or she has a résumé.
- Candidates should have a separate résumé for each of their three to five job objectives.
- Résumés need continuous revision, in light of interview experience, to add a new emphasis or to list forgotten achievements.

- Résumés should be expressed in language familiar to the interviewer and achievements should be stated in short phrases or sentences.

Many books and kits are available for further reference. An example is Briley and Porter's *Résumé Kit and Job Search Guide*.[9] Commercial résumé preparers also are available for consultation. The fee varies from $50 to $400. The outplacement counselor provides this consultation service as part of the process. In fact, outplacement counselors monitor the résumé writing carefully. We could cite horror stories of candidates sending out poorly constructed résumés that undermined their credibility. Résumés are too important to the job campaign and to the candidate's self-confidence to be left to haphazard quality control.

SUMMARY

During job targeting at least three job targets are listed that most closely match the candidate's skills, needs, wants, and values. Candidates then choose the most attractive job arenas in which to conduct their job search. The third task in job targeting is to write a résumé for each job objective. Two basic types of résumés are used in the job campaign—a chronological listing of experiences as they developed, and a listing of achievements by job functions or skills. Another type is a combination of chronological and functional formats. A brief list of achievements is called a "Qual Brief" résumé.

NOTES

[1] U.S. Department of Labor, *Dictionary of Occupational Titles* (Washington, D.C.: U.S. Superintendent of Documents, 1977).

[2] U.S. Department of Labor, *1982–83 Occupational Outlook Handbook* (Washington, D.C.: Superintendent of Documents, 1982). The handbook is updated every two years.

[3] U.S. Department of Labor, *Guide for Occupational Exploration* (Washington, D.C.: Superintendent of Documents, 1979). All job titles in the U.S. are classified into twelve areas of worker interest and are coded to the *Dictionary of Occupational Titles*.

[4] G. D. Gottfredson, J. L. Holland, and D. K. Ogawa, *Dictionary of Holland Occupational Codes* (Palo Alto, CA: Consulting Psychologists Press, 1982).

[5] *U.S. News & World Report,* 31 May 1982, p. 13. (Highest incomes are listed for 40 geographically distributed cities in the U.S.)

⁶Special for *USA TODAY,* Jan. 20, 1983, p. 1, "Salaries on Upswing for Mid-level Managers."

⁷R. Lathrop, *Don't Use a Résumé* (Berkeley, CA: Ten Speed Press, 1980).

⁸W. Cohen, *The Executive's Guide to Finding a Superior Job* (New York: AMACOM, 1978).

⁹T. S. Briley and J. W. Porter, *Résumé Kit and Job Search Guide* (Palo Alto, CA: Mayfield Publishing Co., 1978).

6

The Job Campaign

Now that job objectives are clarified, résumés are completed, arenas are narrowed, and networks are functioning, candidates can focus on their job campaigns. In the final tasks of outplacement counseling—the job search and the final job selection—five key strategies are covered:

- Informational interviews (to discover required skills, qualifications, and hiring practices).
- Making telephone calls (to obtain interviews).
- Writing personal campaign letters (to obtain interviews).
- Developing self-marketing tactics (to develop networks and to use libraries, newspapers, search firms, and employment agencies).
- Developing effective interview techniques (to get the job).

Persevering with the job campaign, especially when jobs are sparse in the market, is the principal difficulty that candidates face. The counselor who provides candidates with the following information will help them maintain high motivation during the job campaign.

THE INFORMATIONAL INTERVIEW

The informational interview is designed for gathering facts about a field in which the candidate is interested, not for finding jobs. Such interviews can be conducted at any time after the self-evaluation stage is completed. Informational interviews are used to

- Check the market for skills required on particular jobs.
- Determine what jobs are likely to be open in an industry.
- Check several industries to determine which of the candidate's transferable skills are needed.
- Widen the candidate's range of acquaintances.

Check the Required Skills

A thirty-eight-year-old retail store worker, Robert T., wanted to go into retail sales. He was asked to check on market requirements by conducting ten informational interviews at three different types of stores. He was to ask the following questions:

- "I am thinking about going into retail sales.
- What skills do you like to see in your salespersons?
- What is the future of this kind of sales work?
- Do you know of any stores in need of a salesperson such as this?
- Before I close this interview, would you give your impression of me as a potential salesperson?"

He did this task so skillfully that he was offered two jobs following his informational interviews.

Find Likely Openings

To determine if jobs were available in the industry, John J., a twenty-seven-year-old chemist, interviewed three different chemical companies. All were hiring only people with a minimum of fifteen years experience. Because of this current situation, he changed his career goal to forensic criminology. He obtained a job that paid a lower salary, but regarded it as an exciting challenge and an opportunity to transfer some of his chemistry skills to a different arena.

Check for Transferable Skills

Lucinda S., a fifty-four-year-old receptionist, wanted to change careers but she did not know what kind of job would be appropriate for her background. After completing her self-assessment, she decided she wanted to work in the enterprising, social, and artistic arenas. She did some informational interviewing in two fields that included travel agencies and shipboard companionship. On the basis of these data, she decided that travel agency work better met her requirements.

Broaden Acquaintanceships

Informational interviews sometimes do not exactly fit the candidate's needs, but they serve to widen networks and increase self-esteem. From our experience we estimate that one out of every ten informational interviews will lead to a specific job placement.

TELEPHONE CALLS

Calls are made to get interviews. Sometimes telephoning is difficult, even for experienced manager candidates who are not accustomed to asking for favors. Role playing a telephone call gives candidates practice and feedback. Candidates should be well primed with knowledge about what they want, market information, and particular company or product information.

After obtaining the contact's name and permission to use the referring person's name, the candidate might say, for example, "My name is _____. Our mutual friend _____ suggested I call you. I'll be in the midst of a career change sometime in the next few months, and after studying your corporation's needs, I have developed a plan I would like to show you on how to increase profits in the _____ department. Is it possible to see you sometime in the next few weeks to show you this plan?" While candidates will couch these ideas in their own language and style, they should be reminded to be direct and brief.

CAMPAIGN LETTERS

Purposes of Personal
Letters

Some placement experts claim that the personal campaign letter gets the job. We say, rather, that personal campaign letters get the attention of prospective interviewers, since the letter cites the reason for contacting the organization, describes the job being sought, and offers a brief statement of qualifications. The personal campaign letter advises the recipient that the writer will call in a week to ten days for an interview appointment.

Types of Letters

Campaign letters are classified as

- Targeted
- Broadcast
- Follow-up

Target letters are sent to friends or network referrals. They may also be targeted to a newspaper ad or a position discovered through hearsay. When this letter is sent to friends, it may include the résumé; sent to strangers, however, it is advisable not to include a résumé or qual brief

```
[company name and address]
----------------
----------------
----------------


Attn:  Mr. --------------
       Director of Administrative Services/Personnel

Dear Mr. ----------------:

       -------------- has suggested that I write you about my seeking an entry-
level management position in the area of marketing.  For the past one and
one-half years I have been in management training with the Bank of -------.

       During that period, my training has been very extensive in both opera-
tions and consumer lendings.  In addition, I have been involved with
special assignments such as:

             · Account Profitability Analysis
             · New Accounts Set Up/Introduction
             · Customer Information File.

       I also believe that my B.S. in Business Administration with emphasis in
marketing can be utilized effectively by -------------------.

       I would appreciate the opportunity of a personal interview with you.  I
will call you within the next ten days to set up an interview date.


                            Sincerely yours,


                            ---------------------


   jy
```

FIGURE 10   Sample targeted letter

at first. Rather, the goal of the letter is just to get attention by pointing out the candidate's qualifications for the desired job. The statement should include that a phone call will follow in a week to ten days. Figure 10 is a sample target letter to be sent to a friend in the network.

Broadcast letters sent to organizations usually should not include résumés or qual briefs, but they should include a short list of achievements, as indicated in Figure 11. Candidates may include something personal that gives hints about who they are, such as, "I have been called a tough manager," or "I am known as the surgeon of our industry," or "I have been called one of the more personable managers." The example in Figure 11 notes that the candidate has studied detailed corporate information that has enabled him to indicate how he might improve productivity. It is important in this detailed study to get the exact names and titles of the addressees. Using salutations like "Dear

```
[company name and address]
------------------
------------------
------------------

Dear Mr. [or Mrs. or Ms.] --------:

    I have studied your P & L Statement and examined your mode of

operation.  As a result I have come up with some ideas on how to upgrade

your productivity.

    You may be interested in a man competent to do Corporate Planning and

Economic Development.  Here are some of my accomplishments:


    . As a liaison officer I represented an electronics corporation
      involving over $150,000 in sales.  I am skilled in management-
      government interface.

    . As an electronics engineer I was among the first to introduce and
      implement Systems procedures, through a management by objective
      approach.

    . As Senior Vice President of a major corporation, I developed programs
      to implement innovative engineering-management, participatory
      management.


    Age 40, married, three children, excellent health, B.S. Electrical

Engineering.  Can you use an executive with these qualifications in your

business?  I will call you within the next ten days.


                              Sincerely

                              ------------------
```

FIGURE 11 Sample broadcast letter from a generalist executive

```
    Dear ----------------:

        I certainly enjoyed the chance to meet with you last week.  I left our
    discussion with ideas about the job that I could do for you.


        You will recall some of the facts we discussed:
        (1)  As a Field Representative for -----------------------
             I increased annual sales by 125% in 5 years.

        (2)  As District Sales Manager of ---------------------,
             I aided management's sales figures by $1,000,000.00 in 2 years.


        I look forward to hearing from you after you and your staff have
    reviewed my resume and our discussion.  I will call within the next two
    weeks for a second appointment.


                                        Sincerely,


                                ---------------------
```

FIGURE 12   Example of an interview follow-up letter

Sir" or "Dear Mr. Manager" is a poor substitute for using real names.
A letter with candidates' address and telephone number clearly
included at the top makes it easy for prospective employers to contact
them.

   Follow-up letters are imperative whether contact is made in person
or by telephone. Candidates should send a letter (such as Figure 12) as
soon as possible after interviews to thank interviewers for their time and
consideration, and to remind them of the positions being sought. A summary statement aims to keep the contact alive, such as "I will be contacting you again in another two to three weeks." Candidates should keep
their contacts alive until the interviewers give the cue to drop them.

HOW TO GET JOB LEADS AND
PLAN EFFECTIVE SELF-MARKETING

One advantage of having a counselor-consultant to help with this entire
process is that candidates can discuss the most appropriate avenues and
timing for job finding.

Sources of job referrals cover a wide range of possibilities. Examples are

- Personal network,
- Professional and trade association meetings,
- Library resources—directories and trade journals,
- Employment agencies and college placement services,
- Newspaper ads and journal job notices,
- Search firms.

Candidates should make a job campaign chart such as the "Plan-Do-Control" model in Table 1. They should list the strategies to be utilized, then decide on implementing tactics, followed by a plan to insure results from the strategy and tactics.

TABLE 1   Examples of the "plan-do-control" model for self-marketing

Plan (strategy)	Do (tactics)	Control (results)
Network	Discover contacts	Letters
	Call friends	Thank you notes
	Make goals	
Ads and Trade Sources	Search or subscribe	Follow-up
	Be persistent	phone calls
	View receptionists as friends	
Search Firms & Placement Agencies (Headhunters)	Choose carefully Authorize résumés	Follow-up
Hunches	Wait for clues	Follow-up
	Listen to self/others	
Group Network	Contact group representative	Follow-up with representative
Library Search	Peruse	
	Business directories	
	Chambers of Commerce	
	Investigate leads, Better Business Bureau	
Attending Professional and Trade Meetings	Register for attendance and circulate	Follow-up
	Apply to placement desk or post bulletin boards	

The Personal Network

A personal network is a list of friends, neighbors, colleagues, work associates, family, classmates, and friends of friends who trust the candidate's integrity and who might provide leads to job openings. Candidates should be urged to start their lists as soon as possible after their termination, for it tends to give them confidence as they begin to realize that many helpful people are ready to offer ideas.

Personal connections.   We are convinced that the network is the most productive way to make campaign contacts. We confirm Bolles'[1] estimate that about 95 percent of the positions sought by executives are filled through the network system. Morin and Cabrera[2] state that it accounts for 70 percent of all jobs accepted.

Networks often lead in circuitous ways to job openings. One of our candidates' acquaintances, for example, was a janitor who often passed the chief executive officer of his firm in the hall. The janitor had the courage to speak to the executive about his friend, the candidate. The executive knew of an opening, sought out the candidate, and made some telephone calls that helped place him with another firm. Each person on the network list may lead to one or two others who know of job leads.

Mary Blakeman, in a Pacific News Service article,[3] indicated that personal connections still determine to a large extent who is hired. She cited San Francisco labor researcher Miriam Johnson's estimates that 65 percent of the work force obtains jobs through personal information. A U.S. Department of Labor study[4] stated that family and friends provide 54 percent of the job leads.

Word-of-mouth methods are preferred by many employers to avoid the crushing load of résumés that come in when positions are advertised through the usual media channels. Many examples could be cited where the informational network gets the word out before the position is advertised formally. Most government organizations operate under strict fair employment practice rules regarding advertisements of positions; but even here, word gets out early to some people.

While informational systems help employers to find candidates with the best personal fit, such systems restrict the number of qualified candidates who are reviewed. The informal system also invites accusations of favoritism and prejudice; yet it persists as the most productive route to job leads.

Network guidelines.   Some guidelines for candidates to be aware of when utilizing networks are

- Make the termination situation clear to the people in the network.
- Clarify present circumstances and tell people briefly of future hopes; for example, "I'm looking for a new career."
- Tell people of time invested in the search process to date (such as the 50 to 100 hours spent choosing objectives and preparing résumés), to confirm serious intent.

- Tell them, when appropriate, about the career planning consultant who is a guide in this crucial career change.
- Ask for names of people who would be suitable contacts. For example, "I am seeking information about the fields of ___, ___, and ___. Whom do you know that I should speak with in order to learn more about possibilities in the field? (This is asking for suggestions about people, not positions.) Network people will respond if they are aware of positions, but they are more likely to refer candidates to friends and associates if they understand that the contact is for gathering information at this point.
- Ask the network people's permission to use their names when calling others to extend the network.
- Thank network contacts and indicate that they will be kept up to date on how things are going.

Candidates expect friends to be glad that they called and that they will offer a letter of introduction or a phone call to an acquaintance. There is a social norm among most subcultural groups that they help one another when they can, especially among friends. The counselor must remind candidates that almost everyone is in such a situation at one time or another in their lives and that people usually are cordial about being of service at this crucial time. It is important that candidates feel this confidence in people, since occasionally they are reluctant to develop their networks. Sometimes, for example, they feel that they are exploiting their friends by asking for help. They also may consider it demeaning to themselves in the eyes of friends and colleagues to be in such a vulnerable position.

Group outplacement counseling and networking. Some outplacement activities are conducted in small groups or combinations of groups with individual counseling. The group format provides a helpful situation where, through a clearinghouse, members pool job leads that they think would be useful to someone in the group. A member of the company can usually manage this clearinghouse function. This person collects and disseminates contacts for possible networking, and organizes all job information for employees facing dismissal. Most large cities have "Over Forty" clubs, or their equivalent, to help middle-aged professionals become reemployed. They operate basically as self-help groups, but they also offer mutual aid and support. The data needed are

- Name of company, address, phone, and function, service, or product;
- Title of available job;
- Indication of whether job is authorized, and closing date for applications;

- Name of hiring authority;
- Salary levels.

Employees cooperate in this group venture by sharing unused job leads that emerged during their own job campaigns. We have observed that this kind of cooperative effort has a salutary effect on the morale of those who are still searching.

Keeping records is essential to an orderly job campaign. It also helps candidates who become discouraged to persevere with the networking task. The worksheets are illustrated in Figure 13. Item (1) is a simple record of contacts. A more complex record is illustrated in item (2), which

(1) Brief Worksheet for Contact Network

Friends' Names	Referral Name of Friend	Phone #	Address	Comments Incl. Date Contacted/Follow-Up

(2) Network Master List

Friend/Contact	Ref. Page	Referral	Ref. Page	Type of Business

(3) Network Contact Record

File name [Cross-referenced]   Network Page No. _____   Card [3 x 5]

Name   _____   Telephone _____
Title   _____   Category _____
Company   _____   Referred by _____
Address   _____

Date	Time	Action

It is easy to see results and to determine at a glance how the candidate's effort is baing expended. A record can be kept also on resources, other than the network. Examples are directories, registers, journals, and papers that provide leads for broadcast letters.

FIGURE 13   Network forms

contains a master list of contacts. It is cross-referenced to information detail on a single network contact item (3). Putting data on cards makes cross-referencing more efficient. It also allows the counselor to see results and determine at a glance how the candidate's effort is being expended. A record can be kept also on other resources such as directories, registers, journals, and papers that provide leads for broadcast letters.

Library Resources

An important, although time-consuming, strategy for candidates is library research. Seattle Public Library, for example, furnishes a special "Directory of Employers for Job Seekers." Other libraries have special sections related to employment information. Library research includes checking local chambers of commerce, better business bureaus, and business associations for leads on growing businesses or unfilled opportunities. Surveys of community needs compiled by these associations offer rich leads to business and professional opportunities. An example is the rapid growth of businesses around the new Trident submarine base on Puget Sound.

State employment security departments have job information dissemination programs, usually through computerized services.

Professional and trade associations are productive sources of job leads. Almost all have newsletters and trade journals that list openings or growth and decline in different geographic areas. Collections of business data such as Standard and Poor or Dun and Bradstreet can be sources of leads. Chapter 6 "Notes" contain additional examples and sources of self-marketing.

Newspaper Advertisements

Candidate strategy should include regular perusal of advertisements, especially in the more extensive local Sunday editions, *The Wall Street Journal*, or *National Employment Weekly*. However, the counselor should caution candidates that ads have limited value when compared with other sources of job leads such as networks, employment agencies, and placement booths at professional meetings. A Department of Labor study[5] revealed that want ads accounted for only 5 percent of the sources of job leads. Careers columnist Joyce Kennedy,[6] on the other hand, uses data from the Employment Management Association's survey of job leads to urge candidates to persist in following help-wanted ads. This ad follow-up strategy calls for submitting broadcast letters, or résumés where requested. As indicated earlier, however, we believe it unwise to give too much information too soon. The preferred strategy is to pique the curiosity of prospective employers so they will request more information in an interview.

Timing is important. Candidates should watch for the continuation of an ad in the same paper, and then toward the end of the week following its appearance, send a letter. The strategy is to get personal attention later, rather than be lost in the flood of résumés and letters the employer receives immediately after the ad appears. The aim is to get an appointment by telephone as soon as possible after the letter is received. Candidates follow this step with the résumé, the interview, and then the follow-up, as already noted.

Perusing the obituary columns, notices of terminations, management changes, and promotion lists in the business section may give clues to vacated positions.

Professional and Trade Association Meetings

Attending professional or trade association conventions or local chapter meetings can be a productive source of job leads. Getting to know the old timers on a social basis can also be a networking aid. Three tactics are helpful to candidates attending professional and trade association meetings: (1) Discussing issues with colleagues at the meetings provides visibility. (2) Parties and social hours at the conventions get the candidates' job campaign message across. (3) Large conventions run placement services that require advance registration. While organized primarily for the entry-level professional, these services also tend to assist those more advanced in their careers or, at any rate, offer opportunities to meet placement representatives from organizations in the candidates' chosen job arenas.

College placement services generally offer assistance to alumni. Private universities, especially, take a lifelong career interest in their graduates. Counselors should remind candidates who are college graduates that they probably have this privilege.

Executive Search Firms

Search firms have been called headhunters, as used by Cohen in his chapter for executives on "How to get a job through a corporate headhunter."[7] We are firmly convinced that candidates should not use headhunters while in the outplacement counseling process. In their anxiety about being unemployed, candidates may impulsively register with search firms. This focuses their attention on early employment prospects, rather than on thorough self-assessments and job searches. As a result, the candidates' interests in the most sound, long-term placements are jeopardized. Search firms work for companies, not for individuals; they are not fee-collecting agencies that represent employees.

Search firms, in our experience, tend to shun the unemployed and show an interest primarily in currently employed executives who might be ready to move. Furthermore, search firms—especially those with reputations as headhunters—do little or no counseling; primarily they perform a paper exchange. Search firms usually are paid a retainer, but when the candidate is placed, they receive a fee—up to one third of the candidate's salary. Consequently, lawsuits arise when a company hires a candidate whose unsolicited résumé was—without the knowledge of the candidate—sent to them earlier by a search firm, which now tries to collect a placement fee. Suits arise also from more than one search firm sending the same résumé.

Therefore, candidates must be cautioned about prematurely handing out their names and résumés to search firms that call them. If the company receives these persistent calls, inform them that candidates are working with an outplacement counselor and that they may be contacted in due time.

There may be a place for search firms at the end of the counseling process, but it should be on the candidate's terms and be appropriately timed. They do place executives, particularly in specialized jobs, but it is not prudent for the candidate to depend on them. Those wishing to utilize executive recruiting services can locate them through the *Directory of Executive Recruiters*.[8] Candidates interested in managerial positions may write for the American Management Association's "Management Information Service" bulletins related to executive employment.[9] It has no placement service but compiles information to assist members who are seeking positions. Professional counselors estimate that only 2 percent of management jobs are filled through search firms.[10]

Another issue is the conflict of interest that results when outplacement counselors also do search placements. Some outplacement counseling firms proudly assert that they are also in the search and placement business. We consider this practice unethical since a firm collects an outplacement fee up front from the employer who discharged the candidate, and an additional fee from the new employer upon placement. This minimizes outplacement counseling functions. The company becomes a thinly disguised search and placement firm that takes advantage of the fact that placement is a lucrative activity.

Employment Agencies

Private employment agencies frequently work with candidates who have fewer qualifications and annual salary aspirations under $20,000. Such agencies usually are regulated carefully by state laws, even though there has been a trend to deregulate the fees, which are considerably less than the fees of search firms and are frequently paid by the employee—usually about a month's salary.

Candidates should be informed that private employment agencies require a contract as well as an application. They should get a copy of the contract to study at home before signing, and should note the length of time they will have to pay the fee, the number of payments, and the finance charges, or late fees. They should also note whether they have the option of interviewing for jobs in which the employer pays the fees, and if they can refuse interviews where the fee is paid by the applicant. Most laws forbid charging up-front fees for registering or sending résumés, so candidates should be sure that they can be charged only if they accept a job.

Fears of Rejection

One of the candidates' key obstacles to persisting with a chosen strategy is the fear of rejection by potential employers. Persistence in the face of long weeks or months of effort is required, especially in recessionary times. Often the candidates will get immediate feedback on whether their leads are going anywhere or not; but usually they get the word from their network referral contact.

Persistent rejection calls for a diagnostic interview with the counselor to determine if the problem is a defect in the strategy, tactics, or manner of interviewing. It is possible, of course, for the problem to reside in the candidates' discouragement and faltering morale. If the former is the case, training in interviewing or phoning may help. Candidates might make calls with the counselor present and then discuss the results. Another method is to use role playing or videotaped simulations followed by discussion and feedback.

If the problem appears to reside in the candidates' attitudes rather than technique, some personal counseling may be in order to help them work through their fears or discouragement. Candidates need to realize that jobs are out there that are not listed. Krannich and Banis[11] estimate that from 60 to 80 percent of all jobs are in the hidden market—those not posted in traditional ways.

Candidates should be advised to reapply with employers that have previously overlooked them. The Employment Managers Association[12] advises that positions sometimes open up again. Most employers do not have retrieval systems for reconsidering applicants; the refiled application will be treated as a fresh application.

JOB INTERVIEW TECHNIQUES

Techniques of interviewing include

- Obtaining the interview,
- Conducting the interview,
- Following up the interview.

Obtaining the Interview

Interviews are obtained by letters and phone calls. Candidates need to approach from fifty to 100 target organizations in the initial phase of the job campaign, which should then be divided into first and second choices. From this many contacts, the candidate should receive three to five possible job offers. The Department of Labor study[13] indicated that direct contact accounted for 31 percent of job leads.

Just compiling this list requires hard work and discipline. The counselor can aid candidates by suggesting, confronting, and training; but candidates must realize that in the final showdown only they can obtain the interviews. The candidates' hard work in listing and prioritizing tends to increase their endurance, confidence, and hope. Although some candidates will start with high enthusiasm, after a month or so of effort they become bogged down with discouragement and self-blame. Counselors should ascertain if this letdown is a lack of reinforcement or reward for efforts, or whether it is a recurrence of delayed grieving. In either case, some time out for personal counseling is in order. At this phase of the process, counselors can help candidates to endure these tedious weeks and months by being supportive also, but there is no substitute for the inner strength and dogged determination of the candidates themselves. Some are even challenged by the tasks and view them as interesting problems to solve.

Attitudes are the key. Viewing the search task as a challenge is important. A positive attitude must be communicated in the request for an interview. Examples of counterproductive, negative attitudes are "I'm not sure you'd want me"; and "I hope you don't feel I'm bothering you too much."

Another example of a self-defeating attitude is the procrastinators who prepare thoroughly but approach the letter writing or the telephone calling with mounting anxiety. They go back to preparing until the next wave of anxiety overwhelms them, and never get into the market. These negative attitudes often have complex motivational backgrounds. While training and supportive counseling can help some, others would do well to seek extended counseling and retraining to eliminate their self-defeating attitudes.

One characteristic of people who are grieving, for example, is that most of the time they want to do nothing. The counselor needs to use all of his or her professional skill to encourage candidates to move along through the process, and should not reinforce any behavior that indicates procrastination. An example is the candidate who gives excuses why he or she cannot move through the job targeting process on schedule. The counselor who listens to these excuses perpetuates them. On the other hand, a discussion of how the candidate can remove obstacles to action or clarify goals, such as writing the résumé, is a productive tactic. Sometimes a quick diagnostic check needs to be made to determine if a skill deficit, such as writing, is involved. Candidates could be ashamed of their poor writing or spelling skills, for example.

A positive attitude is illustrated in the following direct approach. "I am presently looking to change my career after twenty-five years in the field of _____. Having checked some of your company's needs, I have chosen to call you to talk about what I can do to improve your processes [or your profits]." It is vital in these statements that candidates not only exhibit a positive and confident attitude, but that they also feature their strengths. If a question of limitations arises, candidates should honestly cite one or two of them and should then indicate how they are working to improve themselves on these points.

Coping with Stressors in Seeking an Interview

If anxiety is experienced in obtaining an interview, there are some simple coping skills that candidates can apply to maintain their composure and optimum functioning:

- To reduce tension, candidates should take several deep breaths, exhale slowly, and silently tell themselves to relax.
- Candidates need to remember that they have much going for them on their list of achievements.
- Candidates might practice before a mirror prior to calling.
- Mental rehearsal is vital to preparation. Using this technique, can-

didates memorize and imagine giving the opening phone statement. They should imagine stating briefly three or four achievements and how they could help the organization; they might also write out other statements that may be necessary, rehearsing them for length and impact.

The key to a candidate's successful interview request is a poised and confident attitude based on mental rehearsal and sometimes on physical rehearsal in front of a mirror. The message should take a maximum of one minute for the opening statement and three minutes for the following statements on achievements, although some flexibility must be allowed to encourage feedback.

If the candidate will focus on similar past accomplishments in which she or he has experienced success, it will help to overcome anxiety about calling for appointments.

Conducting the Interview

The successful interview is a carefully prepared and orchestrated event. While it is not possible to rehearse such an interview precisely, there are some guidelines that could be suggested to promote confidence:

- Be aware of personal strengths and limitations (since these are invariably discussed).
- Be prepared for standard questions asked by interviewers (as illustrated in the list that follows).
- Mentally rehearse key questions and imagine answers before the interview, especially descriptions of two or three main achievements.
- Check the résumé and keep in mind achievements and how they relate to corporate needs.
- Check the library for facts in order to become well acquainted with the organization.
- Check personal appearance. The usual rules of good grooming apply. Conservative and neat dress are expected.
- Avoid smoking or smart remarks in the outer office.
- Carry the résumé in one's pocket; it should usually not be shown until the end of the interview. It is not a good idea to carry a briefcase.
- Look ahead during the interview, maintain eye contact, and let the body assume a natural, relaxed pose to avoid awkward postures. Body language is revealing.
- Think enthusiasm and confidence.

- Roll with the interviewer. The interview is a kind of natural conversation. For example, if the interviewer wants to talk about personal issues, neither cut him or her off abruptly nor behave in a manner that is too friendly. Keep the focus on the job, yet be flexible enough to follow the leads of the interviewer.
- Strive for balance between overselling and being too direct and honest. Be confident, but admit any lack of knowledge and state clearly what needs to be known.
- Avoid, as a general rule, discussions of politics, religion, or company personalities. If asked, however, it is important to give short, forthright opinions. Do not play judge in an interview, such as criticizing the company or the interview.
- When referring to networks, ascertain how well the interviewer knows a network friend before dropping the name and comments.
- Follow up on the results of the interview. This is an important part of the process. Consultation with the counselor is helpful at this point.

Additional suggestions for planning and conducting interviews may be found in Medley's *Sweaty Palms: The Neglected Art of Being Interviewed*,[14] Knight's *How to Interview for That Job and Get It*,[15] and Ryckman's *How to Pass the Employment Interview*.[16]

Common Interviewer Questions

Questions commonly asked and topics usually covered by interviewers follow. This list was adapted from a compilation of the Resource Center staff of the Weyerhaeuser Company.[17] These fifty commonly asked questions overlap some, but they will be helpful in briefing candidates on the wide range of possibilities. The list should also help prospective interviewers to cover areas of significance to a job.

1. Why did you choose this particular work?
2. What are your career plans?
3. What do you know about our organization?
4. What are your qualifications that make you feel confident you will be successful in this job?
5. What do you think determines a manager's progress on the job?
6. What personal qualities determine success in your field?
7. What kind of supervisor do you prefer?

8. What have you learned from most jobs?
9. How long do you expect to work here?
10. What are your major limitations?
11. Define teamwork.
12. What job would you choose if you were entirely free to choose.
13. What kinds of people do you find difficult to get along with?
14. What jobs have you enjoyed most? Least? Why?
15. What are your special assets and abilities?
16. What type of work interests you most?
17. What are some disadvantages to your chosen field?
18. What job tasks have not come up to your expectations? I would be interested in those tasks you had hoped and planned to accomplish but were not able to do so—some disappointments. Tell me about them.
19. How effective a planner and decision maker are you? How do you approach the planning process? and deciding tasks?
20. Most of us can think of an important decision we would make differently if we had an opportunity. I am interested in examples of that kind of experience you have had. What is the biggest mistake you have made?
21. What qualities contribute to your effectiveness as a supervisor?
22. From an opposite perspective, what would be obstacles to your supervisory effectiveness?
23. What type of supervisor elicits your best performance?
24. How would you go about motivating employees?
25. Please give me examples of how you have been or might not have been effective in relating with other employees.
26. Some people are impatient and quick tempered. How would you characterize yourself?
27. How do you feel about the progress of your career?
28. What are your future aspirations?
29. What did you find most challenging about your past job?
30. Tell me about yourself.
31. What are your feelings about your past job?
32. How did you get along with your manager?
33. Where do you rank your last job with others you have held? Why?
34. How many hours do you think people should devote to their work each day?
35. What do you think are the chief strengths and limitations of your supervisor?

36.   What are your goals in life?

37.   Where do you want to be in ten years professionally?

38.   What makes you think that you are qualified for this job?

39.   What questions do you have about us?

40.   What kind of student were you in school? What were your successful subjects? Less successful?

41.   How would you describe your previous job—your duties? How do they relate to this position?

42.   What types of [computers, office machine, and so on] can you operate?

43.   What kinds of people did you associate with on your job?

44.   Were these encounters positive or negative?

45.   How much freedom to make decisions did you have on your last job? How did you use it?

46.   Tell me about yourself in relation to this job—what do you want from your next position?

47.   If you came to work for this company, what kinds of problems would you anticipate? How might you cope with them?

48.   What duties of your past job did you prefer? Why did you leave?

49.   What questions did you expect that I have not asked?

50.   Why were you fired?

Some general things the interviewer may ask or discuss are

Work Experience

1.   Responsibilities and duties of present and previous positions.

2.   Work demands: precision, quantity, reaction to emergencies, dealing with people, creativity, supervision.

3.   Jobs liked and disliked.

4.   Reasons for changing jobs, terminations, continuity of employment, reasons for gaps in employment.

5.   Evaluation of past supervisors, associates, and managers.

6.   Reasons for choosing one's occupation; type of work duties, responsibilities, salary, work demands preferred.

Education—Training

1.   Schools and colleges attended, subjects, grades, degrees and honors.

2.   Extracurricular activities, summer and part-time jobs.

3. Reasons for choosing school, subjects, and activities.

Other Activities

1. Avocational activities; reasons for choosing and time spent.
2. Participation in social and community groups; reasons for choice, and leadership.
3. Reading and study of subjects not connected with present work.
4. Military record; service, assignment, rank, reactions.

Health

1. Sick leave record and reasons.
2. Medical and surgical care—present and past.
3. Present health of family.
4. History of alcohol or nonprescriptive drug abuse.

Here are four broad interview leads that are likely to be explored, whether the candidate is an MBA, Ph.D., or recent high school graduate.

1. What do you want to do?
2. Why do you want to work for us?
3. Tell me about yourself.
4. What questions do you have?

Becoming the "Interviewing Interviewee"

Candidates are as much interviewers as are representatives of the company. Candidates need to watch for cues and remain alert to the concerns of the interviewer—such as questions related to the organization, or personal issues raised—and to ask a question or make a comment related to that concern. One of the authors, for example, called upon a purchasing agent during his early days of selling for Republic Steel. As a young, enthusiastic salesman he kept the conversation on Republic products. After ten minutes the agent stopped to point out to the young salesman that the agent had given him three clues to a situation he had hoped to talk about. The salesman had missed the opportunity to inter-view the interviewer.

Interview Follow-Up

A follow-up letter of acknowledgment should be sent, which reviews the interview in a sentence or two and adds pertinent points, as cited earlier in Figure 12. Even if there appears to be little hope about the outcome of the interview, it should be remembered that the interviewer needs qualified candidates as much as they need jobs. Candidates must have faith in the process even if they lack confidence in the interviewer.

Follow-up letters should suggest a call for another appointment after initial material has been reviewed. This strategy keeps the candidate's case before the interviewers until clear signals indicate that they prefer to stop the contact.

Discussion of Salary

The candidate must prepare carefully for the salary discussion by clearly understanding the needs and future plans of the organization. It also helps to have the facts about current salary offerings for different levels of responsibility. Some of these data come from the job interview itself, so it is well if the candidate does more listening than talking.

Typically, the interviewer will ask the candidate what salary he or she wants. A recommended response is something like, "Well, I am mak-ing ____ in my present work, but I am really looking for a challenge at this point. So, I'm open to negotiation on the salary." If the salary offered appears too low, some response such as, "Oh?" is noncommittal. Then the candidate can ask to wait for a few days before responding. It is not desirable to try any kind of power play or pit one company against another on salary offers.

Candidates need to be patient and listen carefully at this stage of the interview. They should not be intimidated by statements such as, "Your qualifications are not quite up to speed and so we will have to start you lower." Instead of getting anxious or defensive, the candidate might respond with a general phrase such as, "Tell me more," which keeps the dialogue going and defensiveness down. Counselors should remind can-didates to think of their strengths at this point and not be shaken by reminders of their limitations.

When discussing salaries, candidates need to raise such issues as bonuses, profit sharing, and other benefits, if they have not been men-tioned. Personal issues that mean much to the candidates and their families should be raised at this point as further justification for salary and benefits expected.

Candidates should be advised to resist the temptation to make quick concessions just to come to a decision. Statements such as, "I need to think about it further," or "I need to put this and other things into the mix before I make a decision," allow the necessary time for consideration of the offer or to plan a counter offer.

Candidates should be reminded that job interviews are meeting points between two interested parties—one in finding the right person for the job and the other the right job for the person. It is a clarifying and negotiating process in which both parties have the same goal—a satisfying and productive relationship.

After the Job Is Landed

It is important that candidates send letters of thanks to all persons contacted during the job campaign, including the network, interviewers, and all those helpful along the way. The letter also serves as a form of feedback to them.

The outplacement counselor also needs to know the location and type of job obtained, salary level, and benefits. This information helps independent consultants to fulfill reporting responsibilities to the sponsoring agency.

PERSEVERANCE IN THE JOB CAMPAIGN

One of the key tasks of candidates, especially in a tight job market, is keeping their spirits up by maintaining their hope and optimism. In the long frustrating months of the job campaign, candidates often become discouraged. They need to realize that they are on a kind of "fishing expedition" in which job offers are proportional to the amount of effort expended. Some candidates expect immediate results and are disappointed when they do not get several offers in response to their first broadcast letters. The following vignettes illustrate some ways candidates have used to spark their perseverance.

Dale G. was ready to give up after trying persistently for over a year to get placed. He consulted with his counselor, who discovered that he conveyed a negative impression in his interviews. They worked together until he found the clue to being more positive in job interviews.

Mary J. was reassured that she was on the right track and that she would need to keep trying a little longer for that top-level job. Discussion of possible obstacles and problems revealed she apparently was conducting the job campaign well.

After four months of looking, Shirley S. and her counselor decided it was best for her to change her career direction. She immediately sought more training.

Gary S., who had always worked for a major corporation, was frustrated after six months of search for a high-level corporate management job. In a burst of creativity he opened a new store as an entrepreneur in a completely different career field.

Rick B. plodded along with occasional periods of depression. He drew on his religious background and used prayer to lift his spirits and to keep the search moving. He finally found a job at half again the salary he had received in his previous job.

Alice T. continued plodding along trying to understand why she was being rejected. She used her counselor for support during these discouraging months and realized that the delay in being placed was due to the tight job market, not personal deficiencies.

In some of these vignettes, the candidates' frustrations led them to reassess their goals and personal attributes and, if necessary, to change career directions. In others, their determination to keep trying was strengthened.

Some candidates do not stick with their outplacement process and immediately launch into a job search. One, for example, took a job right away because his wife was unemployed. A two-year follow-up revealed that he was doing quite well. He gambled and won without going through much of the counseling and planning process. On the other hand, another candidate took the first position he could find because he could not face the stigma of "looking for a job." After six months he had to resign because it was the wrong job for him. He went back to complete the outplacement counseling process before launching another job search.

There are candidates who fail at the interview stage, not because of discouragement, but because they cannot function well due to personal problems. It is important that the grieving process be resolved and that family, financial, and personal problems be cleared up through intensive work with counseling specialists.

SUMMARY

The job campaign contains six strategies leading to placement: Conducting informational interviews, placing phone calls, writing personal job campaign letters, developing and utilizing a personal network, initiating marketing tactics, and practicing job interview techniques. Specific job referrals are obtained from search firms, personal networks, newspaper ads, and employment agencies. Most job leads are obtained through the candidate's personal network.

NOTES

[1]Richard Bolles, *What Color Is Your Parachute?* (Berkeley, CA: Ten Speed Press, 1980).

[2]W. Morin, and J. Cabrera, *Parting Company* (New York: Harcourt-Brace-Jovanovich, 1982).

[3]Mary Blakeman, "Personal Contacts Still Keys to Job Hunt," Pacific News Service, reported in University of Washington *Daily,* 2 December 1982.

[4]U.S. Department of Labor, *Career Threshholds,* Vol. 1, Research Monograph 16, Tables 4.13–4.5, 1980. Basis for a training package on how people find jobs.

[5]Ibid.

[6]Joyce Kennedy, "Overlooking Help-Wanted Ads Is a Big Mistake," Syndicated Column "Careers," *Seattle Times,* 5 December 1982.

[7]W. Cohen, *The Executive's Guide to Finding a Superior Job* (New York: Amacom, 1978).

[8]L. Kennedy and R. Kennedy, *Directory of Executive Recruiters* (Fitzwilliam, N.H.: Business Publishers, 1980).

[9]AMA Management Information Service, *Executive Employment Guide* (New York: American Management Association, 135 W. 50th St.).

[10]Bolles, *What Color Is Your Parachute?*

[11]R. L. Krannich, and W. J. Banis, *High Impact Letters and Résumés* (New York: Progressive Concepts, 1982).

[12]Employment Managers Association, as reported in *U.S. News & World Report,* 13 December 1982, p. 82.

[13]U.S. Department of Labor, *Career Threshholds.*

[14]H. Medley, *Sweaty Palms: The Neglected Art of Being Interviewed* (Belmont, CA: Lifetime Learning Publications, 1982).

[15]D. Knight, *How to Interview for That Job and Get It* (Ennersville, IN: Commercial Printing Service, 1976). Lists rules of interviewers and techniques for handling the interviewee as a candidate.

[16]W. Ryckman, *How to Pass the Employment Interview* (Homewood, IL: Dow Jones-Irwin, 1982).

[17]Barbara Wyatt, *Questions Commonly Asked at Job Interviews* (Kent, WA: Compiled by the staff of the Resource Center of Weyerhaeuser Company, 1982).

Resources

Samples of Professional and Trade Association Publications That List Job Openings

Banking: *Bank Marketing* (monthly), Bank Marketing Association, 309 W. Washington St., Chicago, IL 60606.

Computer technology/application: *Computerworld* (weekly), Patrick J. McGovern, Publisher, 375 Cochituate Road, Framingham, MA 01701.

Metallurgy: *Metal Progress* (monthly), American Society for Metals, Metals Park, OH 44073.

Chemical engineering/application: *Chemical and Engineering News* (weekly), American Chemical Society, 1155 Sixteenth St. N.W., Washington, D.C. 20036.

Psychology/professional: *Monitor, American Psychological Assn.*, 1200–17th St. N.W., Washington, D.C. 20036.

Self-Marketing and Job Targeting Resources

Business Information Resources. (Published by University of California Press, Berkeley and Los Angeles, CA, 1976).

 Comprehensive information on methods of locating facts; locating information on companies, organizations, and individuals; basic U.S. and foreign industrial statistics sources; U.S. business and economic trends sources; and chapters on individual businesses, that is, accounting, computers, banking, insurance, and real estate.

Dunn & Bradstreet's Million Dollar & Middle Market Directories, 2 volumes, Volume 1. (Published by Dunn Marketing Services, 3 Century Dr., Parisippany, NJ 07154.)

 Besides eligible industrial concerns, the directories list utilities, transportation companies, banks and trust companies, stockholders, and mutual and stock insurance companies, as well as wholesalers and retailers. Alphabetical by company name, with address, telephone number, sales volume, number of employees, stock trading information, nature of business, CEO, chairman of the board, board members, and executives.

Dunn & Bradstreet International Businesses. (Published by Dunn & Bradstreet International Ltd., 1 World Trade Center, New York, NY 10048, 1980.)

Principal international businesses in four languages (English, French, German, and Spanish). Lists: complete business name and address, parent company, sales volume, number of employees, import/export indicators, SIC (Standard Industry Classification number), line of business, cable/Telex information, CEO name and title.

Encyclopedia of Business Information Sources. (Published by Gale Research Co., Book Tower, Detroit, MI 48226, by Paul Wasserman and others, 1980.)

Alpha listing of industries, with subheadings that list: Encyclopedias and dictionaries; handbooks and manuals; bibliographies; abstract services and indexes; statistics sources; price sources; almanacs and yearbooks; financial ratios; general works; and on-line data bases.

F & S (Funk & Scott) Indexes. (Published by Predicasts, Inc., 11001 Cedar Avenue, Cleveland, OH 44106, updated weekly with quarterly cumulations.)

Lists recent articles on firms and products, source materials (magazines and journals) on specific industries and businesses, Alpha guide to SIC numbers. Section 1—Industries and products arranged by major industry groups, Section 2—Companies arranged alphabetically.

F & S Index of Corporations and Industries (Pub. same as above). Lists published articles by industry and company name. Also updated weekly.

MacRae's Blue Book, 5 volumes. (Published by McRae's, 100 Shore Drive, Hinsdale, IL 60521, 1980, 87th ed.).

Volume 1—Corporate index (company name and address), plus capital ratings, and trade name index; Volumes 2 through 4—Products classified; Volume 5—Manufacturers' product catalogs.

Moody's Manuals (Published by Dunn & Bradstreet Corp., 99 Church St., New York, NY 10017.)

Industrial: Complete coverage section: companies prominent in American industry.

Bank & Finance: Complete coverage section: companies prominent in American finance.

OTC Industrial: Full measure coverage section: more companies prominent in American industry.

Transportation: Complete coverage section: prominent railroad companies.

Municipal & Government: City, town, and state governments.

Standard & Poor's Corporation Records. Very regular updates, 9–10 volumes. (Published by Standard & Poor's, 25 Broadway, New York, NY 10014.)

Alphabetical listing of companies with capitalization; corporate background; line of business; stock date; earnings and finances; an annual (or quarterly) report; and consolidated balance sheet.

Standard & Poor's Industry Surveys, 2 Volumes. (Published by Standard & Poor's Corp., 345 Hudson St., New York, NY 10014.)

Lists of stock by industry, for comparison of a company within its own industry.

Standard & Poor's Register of Corporations, Directors, & Executives, 3 volumes. (Published by Standard & Poor's, 25 Broadway, New York, NY 10014.)

Volume 1—Corporate listings (approximately 37,000), alphabetically by company name (Incl. address, and so on), officers, exchange on which company's stock is traded, SIC (Standard Industry Classification number), annual sales, number of employees and nature of business. Volume 2—Individual listings for directors and executives (approximately 74,000); also officers and partners, and so on. Volume 3—Indexes: SIC by industry; SIC by number; *geographical listings* of companies in an area; obituary of executives; new individual additions; and new company additions.

Thomas' Register of American Manufacturers & Catalog File, 16 volumes.
Volumes 1–8—Products and services listed alphabetically.
Volumes 9–10—Company names (address, phone, and so on), plus branch offices, capital rating, and company officials.
Volumes 11–16—Catalogs of companies.

Walker's Manual of Western Corporations. (Published by Walker's Corporation, 5855 Naples Plaza, Suite 101, Long Beach, CA 90803, 1980.)
Indexes are alphabetical, by geographical location, and by industrial classification. Plus address; market; business; comment by management; revenues and operating income; principal facilities; acquisitions; sold, liquidated, and consolidated; and specific stock information.

The Wall Street Journal Index, annual, with monthly updates. (Published by Dow Jones & Co., Inc., 22 Cortlandt St., New York, NY 10007.)
Section 1—Corporate news by company and person's name.
Section 2—General news by person and general topics.
Brief abstract of all articles for year, and how to find full article.

The Wall Street Journal National Business Employment Weekly. (Published by Dow Jones, as above.)
A weekly compilation of career-advancement positions from the four regional editions of *The Wall Street Journal.* Also available at many newsstands.

7

How to Relate Inplacement Counseling with Outplacement Counseling

We have stated frequently that inplacement counseling is an alternative to outplacement counseling. Inplacement counseling includes counseling for

- Up, down, and lateral placement,
- The marginal (or troubled) employee,
- Personal problems in the employee assistance program,
- Retirement options,
- Pretermination planning and possible retraining,
- Better marginal and technical fit in a growing organization,
- Awareness of managerial and technical skills as part of a total career planning program
- Continuing education

In this chapter we will describe these inplacement counseling services and propose how outplacement counseling can be done internally by human resource management staff. The outplacement counseling methodology already detailed in earlier chapters is applicable to inplacement counseling, especially the self-evaluating, job targeting, and self-marketing functions.

HUMAN RESOURCE MANAGEMENT SERVICES AND INPLACEMENT COUNSELING

The inplacement counseling services just listed are only one component of the total human resource management program, which may also include

- Selection and staffing,
- Compensation and benefits,
- Performance evaluation,
- Training and development,
- Organizational development,
- Job and systems design,
- Human resource planning and research,
- Outplacement counseling.

Integrating Inplacement with Outplacement Counseling Services

One of the key tasks of human resource managers is integrating inplacement counseling with outplacement services. Executives need a hierarchy of options when considering termination of an employee. In times of retrenchment, especially, managers need a wide range of choices to meet the challenges of maintaining productivity while retrenching. Some of these challenges include

- Restructured businesses,
- Reorganized economies,
- Shifts in career patterns and the nature of work,
- Variations in managerial styles,
- Variability in managerial productivity.

We have found that the challenges just listed persist in a retrenching as well as a growing organization. We also discovered that the same counseling tools can be used in both retrenchment and growth strategies. Policy makers who have established a planned human resource management program, and who have instituted attractive management policies, can expect that this inplacement program will

- Attract competent people,
- Discourage disillusioned, but competent, people from leaving,
- Reduce "pirating" of capable employees by competitors,
- Discover and retrain marginally productive employees,
- Improve productivity generally through career planning and training,
- Enhance organizational morale.

An example of a business plan developed by W. H. Levings to accomplish these outcomes is presented in Appendix A. This plan gives the rationale for inplacement counseling, outlines the consultative function, and cites the advantages of instituting such a program.

Relationships of Inplacement to Outplacement Counseling

To clarify the relationships between inplacement and outplacement counseling, we present the human resource management functions and processes in Figure 14. At the top of Figure 14 some of the human resource management programs (I) that occasion consultation are presented. The usual pattern is managerial consultation from internal or external specialists. Out of these consultations the various options for disposition of the employee in question emerges. A management decision (II) is made and implementation is directed to the internal coordinator (III). This coordinator manages the various possibilities reflected in Figure 14.

Examples of Inplacement Counseling at Work

One of the authors has been engaged as a consultant in a large Western manufacturing plant. The goal was to facilitate management decisions about who was to be outplaced and how the remaining employees could be better fitted through inplacement counseling. The internal coordinator, a member of the human resources management team, implemented decisions of the line managers to study and recommend the best form of action, from termination to retraining. The internal coordinator, working with the external consultants, made the first-order decisions reflected in Figure 14: to contract with an external outplacement firm, retire, refit, or retrain.

For some employees with performance problems the above four initial placement options did not seem appropriate, especially since the company wanted to retain their services as long as possible. So, the coordinator recommended to some employees that they seek confidential individual counseling as an alternative to termination. Some of these counseling functions are performed by in-house staff, such as the Employee Assistance counselors; but in this instance the counseling was done by external consultants because of the bearing of confidentiality to employee trust. Within the ethical limits of confidential counseling, however, the counselor works with the coordinator in the mutual interests of the person and the organization. The external counselor helps the person to evaluate

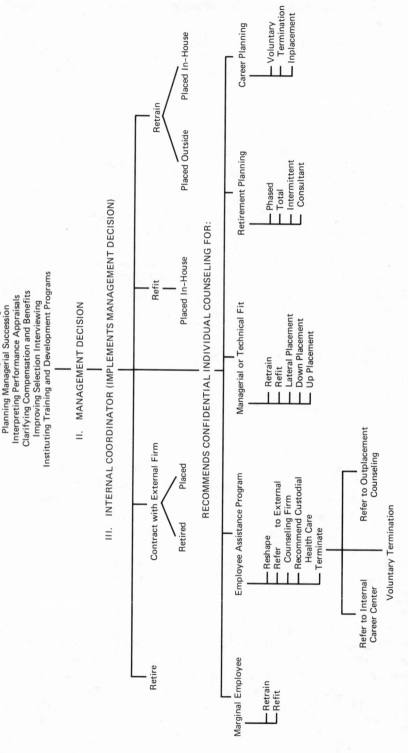

FIGURE 14 The relationship of inplacement and outplacement counseling

performance data and his or her own feelings, while the coordinator and the line management teams take responsibility for any termination actions.

Another example was the instance of a small firm where the consultant recommended retraining. The process took the following general form:

- The human resource management staff assesses the employee,
- Counselor assists employee to assess himself or herself and to interpret company data.
- In the counseling process employee decides if retraining is attractive and feasible.
- Employee requests retraining.
- If coordinator does not concur, then employee, counselor, and coordinator confer until action plan is satisfactory to the employee and the company.
- Coordinator arranges training after all concur.
- Counselor follows up to determine progress under the new retraining plan.
- Counselor meets with coordinator to determine if the organization's goals are being achieved under the new plan.

A similar program could be planned in the case of a refitting. The coordinator uses the data from performance appraisals to motivate behavior change, thus keeping the judgment and push for reshaping on managerial shoulders.

The Case for Inplacement Counseling

While outplacement appears at first to be a painful, but efficient, way to deal with personnel problems, it often turns out to be a counterproductive action for both the organization and the individual. The organization loses valuable skills and experience, and the employee who is terminated must experience the trauma of unemployment and the strain of a new job search.

The effects of unemployment are well documented. In a study of unemployment effects by Morris-Vann,[1] school-aged children suffered from irritability, daydreaming, and depression that interfered with their school achievement. Riegel[2] documents the toll that unemployment takes on individuals, as reflected in the level of health, family harmony, alcoholism, and drug abuse. As the unemployment rates rise, so do spouse abuse, delinquency, and divorce. Apart from these severe conditions associated with unemployment, the toll is high in low self-esteem, fear, discouragement, and boredom.

As a staff exercise at Executive Services Associates we discussed a number of outplacement candidates in terms of the question, "What if the corporation had an inplacement counseling service as an alternative to their outplacement counseling program? How likely is it that this person would have been continued rather than terminated?" During this post mortem discussion the staff decided that the majority of these particular candidates probably would *not* have been terminated, barring those terminated for primarily economic reasons.

Humberger found on his 1982 trip to Europe that French businesses have little need for outplacement services because of the new law that requires every corporation to have a human resources program. This law reinforces the present policy of not terminating an executive unless it is for extreme breaches of policy or morality. Similarly, in Asian countries, personnel are retained as members of the "company family" as long as they wish, although usually in different roles. Thus, cumulative expertise is traded for job security.

Problem managers.   The Sears study, cited earlier, is an example of managerial flaws leading to terminations that were largely preventable. Humberger's study,[3] using the Myers-Briggs Type Indicator (an inventory of personality types) and judgments about underlying causes for 102 terminations, suggested that appropriate human resource counseling services would reduce the need for terminations. While Humberger's results varied for different job categories, 37 percent of all the terminated candidates indicated that they were unhappy on their jobs. Included were 14 percent judged by the counselor to have negative personal characteristics, emotional problems, or conflict with supervisors. The remaining two thirds were terminated mainly for economic reasons. Of the 37 percent unhappy on their jobs, half indicated that the reasons were inadequate challenge and emotional conflicts related to the job. These data support our earlier claim that a better program of selection and confidential inplacement counseling would find these "problem" people earlier; and if the problems were not remediable, at least many would leave voluntarily or would be terminated before a major crisis.

Job dissatisfaction rates high as a reason for voluntary and involuntary terminations. Low productivity and reduced motivation are the primary consequences of dissatisfaction. Enlightened management practice has attended to the causes of such employee dissatisfaction and has developed resource management programs to alleviate them. These causes range widely from complaints about lack of participation in management to deficient company benefits. The basic principle is that all employees, from executives to the lowest-paid hourly workers, expect recognition, respect, and affirmation. The current emphasis on participatory management and the popularity of quality circles attest to this basic principle. Growing reports of job burnout also indicate that employees were consistently ignored and unappreciated. This thorny issue of job satisfaction and productivity suggests that inplacement counseling and management training should be high-priority functions in any organization.

INPLACEMENT COUNSELING SERVICES AS ALTERNATIVES TO OUTPLACEMENT COUNSELING

Career Planning Programs

Counseling in management development programs has been part of the corporate scene for many years, but the idea of attending to the career planning needs of older employees in general is a new emphasis that fits the current trends in lifelong career development. Waltz[4] has outlined specific guidelines for organizations wishing to design career development programs in business and industry. He makes a strong case for providing career counseling for all employees to keep the right person in the right job.

Humberger[5] has developed a program of career continuation for executives. His program focuses mainly on executives over age fifty-five who are planning their next twenty-five years. The emphasis is on wholeness and integration, long-range planning, and the pursuit of meaning. The activities are designed to counter the developmental problems that plague middle age, such as boredom, apathy, fatigue, and low challenges. The focus is not on coping and survival for the depressed, burned out, and sickly executives, but on renewal of energy and productivity. There is also the challenge to prevent troubles for the already well-functioning person. The program promotes awareness of values and optimal distribution of time among work, leisure, and family activities. This program projects into retirement and views retirement as another stage in career/life planning. Some examples of such retirement pursuits are listed later under retirement options.

Career continuation counseling. In a carefully run career continuation program, managers are consulted routinely about their future with the organization. This exploration contains discussions about possible changes in the employee's career direction, updating of skills to maintain competence, or desired changes in attitude. Possible termination is not discussed during these routine assessments or performance evaluations; but the subtle threat is there, nevertheless.

If the possibility of separation arises later because of inability or refusal to change, at least the person can be presented with a range of possible actions. For example, offers of down placement or lateral placement may be possible. If these options do not appear to be available or attractive, then consultation regarding voluntary separation is the next choice. Several options arise at this point, such as early retirement (if eligible) or some kind of negotiated resignation. Thus, involuntary termination comes at the end of a string of options.

The options just described reduce some of the potential pain of a sudden termination and involve the person in the decision-making process. Counselors specialized in career continuation can be helpful consultants to executives as they proceed through the various options with their employees. Legal counselors are essential to this process also, since accusations of age discrimination lurk behind every stage in this decision-making process.

Facing change. Part of career continuation is to help employees to grow with the organization and to plan their careers as part of the organization's growth. But a significant aspect of career continuation is the possibility of such a career spanning several types of organizations and locations. Renewal is often helped by change, hence the popularity of sabbatical leaves in academe and increasingly in business and government.

People sometimes feel intuitively that the time has come for a move. Without the support of a career counseling program, however, the person often is anxious and is not likely to change. So, they typically go bumbling along another five years, or until terminated involuntarily. Candidates occasionally tell us that they knew their termination was imminent. One said, for example, "I knew this was coming; I should have sought a change five years ago; I've been going downhill since that time." An adequate career planning program can deal forthrightly with this issue.

Planning. While there are many aspects to this complex topic of career continuation, the principal idea is long-range planning for achieving one's personal goals in the organization. This plan includes how one's work life is to be enriched and updated, and how leaves of absence, vacations, and retirement are to be phased into this plan. It could include consideration of pretermination planning when it is agreed that leaving the organization would be best for all concerned.

Additional considerations are how one's spouse or partner is to be involved in the planning, how one deals with change and aging, and finally how one faces disability and death. The idea is not that we plan our adult lives precisely, or that we think we can always control our lives on our own terms. The point of planning is that we make it more likely that our goals will be achieved with a higher level of satisfaction and productivity than if we used a strategy of muddling through, or grasping fearfully at work tasks as the main source of our life satisfaction.

Retirement Programs

Retirement is a special variation on career continuation, but it is treated as a separate topic in this chapter because of its central relationship to outplacement and inplacement counseling. Early retirements are being viewed increasingly as an alternative to layoff. This option has spurred considerable interest among organizational officers and employees alike because of retirement and age discrimination laws.

Early retirement. Early retirement, sometimes called the "golden handshake," is not a popular idea with many employers because of its legal and financial pitfalls. It has overtones of status, and for some people, offers an attractive solution to an unsatisfactory job. "Early" is interpreted to mean leaving before the conventional retirement age of sixty-five, usually after fifty-five. Some corporations are permitting retirement at forty-five, allegedly to make way for a younger team or to cut pension costs legally. Increasingly, business and government are dropping minimum ages for early retirement and providing benefits as if the person had retired at sixty-five. In spite of increasing longevity and suspension of mandatory retirement rules, fewer than one man in five, and one woman in ten, remains in the work force until age sixty-five.[6] These Department of Labor data indicate also that the number of Americans opting for early retirement has been increasing.

In some programs, even if the job is satisfactory, the financial terms make early retirement attractive enough to opt for another career or long-awaited leisure. For others, it is a risky launching into a rash of financial and psychological unknowns. Early retirement is one option that should be investigated by the employee and spouse before making the final plunge. The problem is that some early retirement plans are offered only for a limited time. That is, the choice must be made before a fixed date, usually only a few months away, and then the option is cut off indefinitely. In this instance of choosing early retirement, long-term security could be sacrificed for short-term gain.

Government and educational institutions have been developing early retirement incentives as a means of saving cash during recessionary times. Corporations have been offering such packages for a long time.

Early retirement has financial benefits for corporations. Such programs, for example, help to make room for new management at substantially lower salaries. This is tricky planning, however, since early retirement for some employees means extensive payments for retirement benefits. Some corporations are discovering that their commitments to pension funding for some early retirees exceed what they paid for salaries during the working years of those employees. Increasing longevity is making such planning difficult for pension fund managers. Hewitt Associates[7] in a 1982 survey found that one in five corporations included early retirement provisions in their cost containment efforts. Corporations vary in their "buy out" incentives (another term for early retirement). Assuming service of about thirty years, most plans do not reduce the pension ceiling, and benefits are equated to age sixty-five. Many plans offer a subsidy of six months' to a year's salary. Most offer full medical coverage also.[8] The existing variations and complexities make counseling employees about early retirement a difficult task. According to Saba,[9] those who find early retirement advantageous are those who have clear goals, know their capabilities, are open to learning, and have a life plan.

An important question is what motivates inquiry into the possibility of early retirement. If it is job dissatisfaction or boredom, it is likely that these same conditions will carry over to retirement.

Financial need is a highly individual matter. Generally, a person accustomed to a fairly affluent life style needs about 60 to 80 percent of preretirement income. Retirement planners generally advise that 50 percent of preretirement income is sufficient to maintain one's present standard of living. Of course, a correction factor for inflation and an emergency fund must be included. Those who take a high risk find that when their sources of income do not add up, they must face up to the challenging task of starting a new career, or at least seek part-time employment.

Phased retirement.   This term describes a gradual movement to full-time retirement. It could take place, for example, as a five-year planned disengagement from full- to part-time employment, or it could mean a program of increasingly longer leaves. The employee usually is laterally placed or down placed to a position that leaves their expertise available to the organization, and yet takes them out of the mainstream of responsibility. Academic organizations, for example, are moving toward various plans from allowing retired faculty to work 40 percent time to age seventy, to taking extended leaves for work in business, industry, or government.

Phased retirement not only allows mutually beneficial consulting and training relationships to exist, but also gives older workers the satisfactions of being mentors to younger personnel. Since most organizations have continuing concerns for community relationships, older employees can perform valuable liaison services with communities. Some older persons have research skills that could be tapped for improving company performance or products. The main point is that phased retirement programs can be mutually beneficial. They offer a graceful and productive alternative to conventional total retirement, shelving, or layoff. It is also another manifestation of the trend toward reducing traditional conflict between corporate and individual interests.

Older employees. Older employees are often a neglected resource. Attention to the development of older employees is prudent management strategy, given the demographic trends in the United States. A U.S. Labor Department study[10] gives projections that show a current peak in the work force between age sixteen and forty-four and then predicts a decline. Thus, economic growth of the future will depend to some extent on the effective utilization of older workers, with less emphasis on exclusive training of younger workers.

A report by the American Society for Training and Development prepared for the U.S. Senate Special Committee on Aging[11] emphasizes the importance of investing in older workers now and viewing them as resources, rather than as liabilities to retire or fire. This report gives an ample rationale and sufficient data to support flexible retirement and retention options for experienced employees.

Retirement activity. Retirement activity choices are increasing. The following list of plans, avocations, education, and leisure pursuits illustrates the numerous possibilities available to retiring employees:

- Interrupted retirement—six months vacation and return to another position in the same or another corporation.
- Phased retirement—lesser responsibilities in the same corporation, phased down over a three- to five-year period.
- Semi-retirement—part-time job in the same or a related corporation (for example, a position as an in-house consultant).
- Consulting retirement—start consulting, production, or service business—part or full time.
- "Dream" retirement—new career, part or full time (for example, "my almost impossible dream").
- Volunteer retirement—pursue community volunteer work.
- Avocation retirement—pursue avocation interests.
- Leisure retirement—retire to pursue leisure interests.
- Ad hoc contract retirement—(for example, contract as manager for same or other corporation for two to five years).

- Educational retirement—return to school to learn new vocation or avocation (for example, skills training or Elderhostel).

Employee Assistance
Programs (EAPs)

Counseling services to help troubled employees with their personal problems that impinge on their productivity have been increasing during the past few years. The cost effectiveness of these services has been demonstrated through reduced absenteeism, sickness and accident claims, and turnover. Kelvin estimates that about 2500 corporations, unions, and nonprofit organizations have employee assistance programs that offer counseling on a wide range of problems, although historically such programs have focused primarily on drug and alcohol abuse. Kelvin estimates also that $40 billion is the price organizations pay for lost productivity, accidents, turnover, absenteeism, and medical costs.[12]

Some examples of large companies with extensive EAPs are U.S. Steel, Sears, International Paper, Amtrak, General Foods, Polaroid, General Mills, Citibank, and J. C. Penney. Amtrak's study in 1978[13] revealed an estimated savings through their EAP of $1 million a year. The indirect costs of employee problems are too staggering even to estimate. In addition, how do we calculate the personal and corporate costs for problems caused by subtle sexual harassment and discrimination on the job? Cunningham's interview for *U.S. News & World Report*[14] reveals the insidious and costly aspects of this problem.

EAPs have been greeted with mixed reactions from employees who appreciate company concern on the one hand, but are skeptical of confidentiality and pressure tactics of supervisors to get them into counseling. The fact that historically EAPs have been euphemisms for alcohol treatment programs gives them a bit of tarnish also. A supervisory training program on how to refer employees goes a long way toward making optimum use of such services. Examples of topics covered in such training programs are

- How to suggest a consultation with an EAP counselor when productivity has been falling,
- How to separate strictly personal problems from emotional complications growing out of boring jobs, inappropriate job placement, job environment problems, organizational weakness, mistimed promotion, or burnout from excessive demands,
- Prevention of problems through consultations with EAP counselors rather than waiting for crises to emerge on the job,

- Cost containment as justification for EAPs,
- Alternatives to a "perform-or-be-fired" attitude.

Awareness of Training
Needs

Managerial awareness.   Training has been the historically popular approach for employee development. This approach has been more proactive than the more reactive EAPs in that training focuses on developing preventive awareness and coping skills rather than solving problems after they develop. Traditionally, training efforts have concentrated on job performance skills and management competencies. Awareness training, communication skills, motivation enhancement, stress management, and health maintenance have been added to increase effectiveness and raise morale.

The purpose of managerial awareness training is to examine the relationship between management practices and attitudes and employee dissatisfaction and turnover. As we stated earlier in this chapter, our experience indicates that at least half of managerial and technical staff terminations are due to top management errors or to policies unacceptable to their subordinates. Awareness programs aim at improving the functional capacity of the organization. The indirect result is likely to be greater employee stability and reduced costs for terminations and replacements.

Employee training and retraining.   Providing employee training is big business for training departments and external consultants. A detailed discussion of this vast subject is beyond the scope of this book, but we wish to emphasize that appropriately timed training events may be alternatives to terminating technically obsolete or personally ineffective employees. Coupled with counseling programs to identify needs and promote training readiness, a skills training program has on occasion reduced the need to terminate people involuntarily. Through confidential counseling we have facilitated resolutions to difficult supervisory relationships that otherwise would have ended in a termination.

Identifying needs for retraining is increasingly important as more organizations see one of their functions as assisting obsolete employees to acquire new skills. This need is apparent over the whole employment spectrum as technological advances, as well as economic changes, make many jobs obsolete or redundant.

Counselors have access to several assessment instruments that pinpoint training needs. An example is the Personal Skills Map[15] that identifies needs for training and personal development in decision making, time management, wellness, personal skills, stress management, drive strength, and sales orientation. In addition, a brief picture is given of the person's level of self-esteem, assertiveness, orientation to change, and empathy. Thus, training programs can be conducted to fulfill specific needs rather than import programs because someone thinks it would be a good idea.

Downsizing and increasing productivity.   Apart from employee development are the continual pressures to cut costs. Therefore, skills in downsizing or managing limited resources are always in demand to make cutbacks in a humane and efficient manner. National Training Laboratories seminars[16] in downsizing are examples of training events that look at the whole picture of retrenchment and holding the line without terminating valuable employees as the strategy of first choice. Looking for creative approaches to increase motivation and productivity, reducing duplication of effort, or eliminating low-priority activities are partial alternatives to massive terminations. Viewing retrenchment as a creative challenge for all personnel rather than as a negative experience that provokes fear and destroys morale is a demanding management challenge.

OUTPLACEMENT COUNSELING BY CORPORATE INTERNAL STAFF

Basic Models

Two models of internal counseling for outplacement are emerging. The first and most common is a general counseling interview with terminated employees supplemented with voluntary training in résumé writing and conducting a job campaign. This service often includes hourly, or nonexempt, as well as managerial and technical personnel. Some examples of firms using this pattern are Dow, Olin, American Can, and Celanese.

The second pattern is a program of full-time specialists who perform services outlined in our earlier chapters—transition counseling, assessment, developing job objectives, and conducting a job campaign. Examples of firms using this complete program are Citibank and General Electric. Most firms with internal counseling services use outside consultants for top executives, difficult cases, and complex problems beyond the skills of staff counselors.

To justify the services of a full-time counselor, an organization would need from forty to fifty candidates a year. This assumes that some of the counselor's time would be devoted to consultations with line managers. Candidates tend to receive an average of about thirty to forty hours of counseling.

Advantages of Internal Corporate Counseling Services

Conducting outplacement counseling internally is desirable because

- It is cost effective.
- It provides convenient reemployment options.
- It can be integrated with other human resource services.

These advantages are well illustrated by the Citicorp example.

The Citicorp example.   At this writing Citicorp[17] offers a model of consulting and counseling services consisting of two counseling specialists and a secretary. Each counselor works with ten to fifteen candidates in various stages at any given time. The counselors consult with line managers on how to conduct termination interviews, package severance benefits, and use internal services or external counseling firms. Some group counseling is conducted for subsidiaries; but the main function is counseling candidates in the main office. The record of these services is such that all candidates find jobs, including 20 percent who return to Citicorp.

In the Citicorp case study, Anderson found that internal counseling saved money—about half the cost of using external outplacement counseling exclusively. Anderson claimed additional advantages such as more control over the process and integration with other services. The visibility of the program was further proof to employees that such a company benefit actually existed. The program was funded by client fees paid from line managers' budgets. Anderson claimed that timing of the service was crucial to success also. The outplacement counselor became involved when the staff relations office assured the counselor that all options had been explored and all grievances were closed. Citicorp's experience indicated that internal and external services working in cooperation was the best model for them. At this writing, then, the internal outplacement service unit was combined with the executive career management unit under an umbrella called "career services."[18] This move provided a comprehensive and cohesive management counseling program.

Limitations of Internal
Services for Outplacement

In our opinion the advantages of internal counseling outweigh the limitations, but awareness of the following issues is essential:

- Conflict of interest between terminating and helping,
- Fears of nonconfidentiality,
- Resistance of executives to counseling by staff specialists.

Conflict of interest.   One of the chief problems in mounting an internal outplacement counseling service is credibility. Employees see through the contradiction between being terminated, often under strained relationships, and being offered the hand of help through outplacement counseling. It is difficult for them to keep termination proceedings and the counseling process separate. Unless these functions are carefully separated, the outplacement counselor is put in an awkward position with the candidate. We see this concern in candidates even in outplacement counseling done by our external consultants. The solution, as inferred in the Citicorp example, is to build the confidence of employees in the outplacement counseling service and limit involvement in the termination process to consulting with executives on general strategy and technique.

Confidentiality.   This issue is related to credibility. Employees must be assured that no information will leak to management about the content of their counseling sessions. As indicated in earlier discussions on ethics, the counselor informs the candidate exactly what will be transmitted to management. Usually this communication is limited to when the person starts and stops the counseling process and the type and location of reemployment.

Resistance of executives.   Outplacement counseling started with external services to top executives and this pattern remains. The following section provides ideas for an integrated program of internal and external outplacement counseling services.

Coordination with External
Consulting Services

A relationship with an external consulting firm is desirable to provide selected outplacement services for executives who would find it awkward to be counseled in-house by former staff subordinates. In addition, there are many possibilities for joint efforts and cross-referral. For example, external consultants could assist with the counseling tasks of working through the anger and grief of termination, or assessment of strengths, with corporate staff picking up on assessing transferable skills and planning the job campaign. It is possible to partition the process into components, although this activity could jeopardize the unity and flow of outplacement counseling.

Organizations could contract for these outplacement counseling components. For example, about 15 percent of counseling time is taken with orientation, grief work, briefing spouses, and preliminary planning. An additional 30 percent of activities revolve around assessment and inventories of skills and accomplishments. Twenty percent more time is devoted to developing job targets, while the remaining 35 percent is consumed in the job campaign.

Individual differences among managers, especially, argue for a tailored program rather than a rigid prescription of services. What we know about the developmental characteristics of middle-aged adults also supports an individualized approach. Thus, a partnership between corporate human resource specialists and external outplacement consultants could provide such a flexible program to meet these varied levels of employees' job campaign needs. This partnership allows for various combinations of group and individual counseling, and for monitoring candidate progress through the outplacement counseling stages. Coordination between human resources development staff and outplacement counseling of hourly and nonexempt staff by industrial relations departments are more possible when some office or organization is looking out for all employees. Thus, some job classes do not fall in the cracks because they are not clearly either white- or blue-collar types.

THE FUTURE OF OUTPLACEMENT COUNSELING

Where is outplacement counseling going from here? Is it a fad that will fade away in a few years? We believe that outplacement counseling is a proven management tool that has a permanent place in human resource management programs. It will continue as a valued service, especially if it is conceived as part of a total human resources management program, and not just an expedient way to get rid of troublesome employees or to assuage corporate guilt. Outplacement counseling is proving to be cost effective and to be helpful to the corporate image.

To grow in professional stature, outplacement counseling must increasingly attract professional counselors who have the qualities noted in Chapter 3. We must never forget that *outplacement counseling is "counseling," not just "placement" or getting the candidates out the back door.* Only with professional counseling will the credibility of the profession grow; and only with professional counseling will candidates grow to high self-esteem and become appropriate corporate fits.

In this book we have described a comprehensive outplacement counseling process and our model of the professional outplacement counselor. While outplacement counseling has been largely a perquisite for terminated executives, we predict that such services will be offered to an increasing number of middle- and lower-level management employees. When we add the technical staff and hourly employees, the opportunities for outplacement services are great.

SUMMARY

Alternatives to termination exist through inplacement counseling programs, which include early and phased retirement, employee assistance services, training, and improved management practices. Outplacement counseling as a counseling tool has a firmly established future in human resource development programs.

Outplacement counseling, when performed by corporate internal staff, is usually a service within a human resource development framework. Internal outplacement counseling programs are increasing. They offer many advantages over contracting with external consultants, although external consultants can work collaboratively with human resource managers on difficult cases and with those in the executive ranks.

NOTES

[1]A. Morris-Vann, *My Dad Is Unemployed* (Falls Church, Virginia: APGA, 1982).

[2]D. Riegle. (U.S. Senator from Michigan reports on research and personal experience with unemployment in Michigan.) "The Psychological and Social Effects of Unemployment," *American Psychologist,* 37 (1982), 1113–15.

[3]F. Humberger, Unpublished staff report. October 1982.

[4]G. Waltz (ed.), *Career Development in Organizations* (Ann Arbor, Michigan: ERIC/CAPS, 1982).

[5]F. Humberger, Unpublished proposal for a program of "Career Continuation for the Mature Executive." December 1982.

⁶E. Shuman, "The Golden Handshake," *Dynamic Years,* March–April 1983, pp. 12–18.

⁷Hewitt Associates survey on early retirement in E. Shuman (ibid.).

⁸Data based on a survey by the management firm of Towers, Perrin, Forster, and Crosby. Reported in E. Shuman (ibid.), p. 15.

⁹A. Saba, vice-president of human resources consulting firm of J. M. Boros and Associates. Reported in E. Shuman (ibid.), p. 15.

¹⁰Reported in Action for Independent Maturity (AIM) feature article, "Human Resource Managers Face Challenge," *AIM Action,* Number 17, Spring 1983.

¹¹ASTD, *Aging and the Work Force: Human Resource Strategies,* report compiled for the U.S. Senate Special Committee on Aging, G233, Dirksen Building, Washington, D.C. 20510.

¹²A. Kelvin, "Corporate Samaritans," *Working Woman,* January 1983, pp. 84–90.

¹³Amtrak study of EAP program reported in A. Kelvin (ibid.).

¹⁴M. Cunningham, "Rumor or Innuendo: A Powerful Harassment," *U.S. News & World Report,* November 29, 1982, pp. 56–57.

¹⁵D. Nelson and G. Lowe, *Personal Skills Map* (PSM) (Bloomington: Bencom, 1982).

¹⁶National Training Laboratories (NTL). Seminar announcement, 1983.

¹⁷L. Anderson, manager of executive outplacement, Citicorp, New York. Unpublished speech to Drake Beam Morin Forum on Outplacement, New York City, Harvard Club, June 9, 1981. (Also published as a brief report, "Inhouse Placement: The Way to Go" in *Employee Relations Bulletin,* October 21, 1981).

¹⁸Correspondence between F. Humberger and L. Anderson-Clark of Citibank, December 1982.

A Business Plan for Executive Services Associates

W. H. Levings, Vice President

The management of human resources is becoming an increasingly important concern in rapidly developing and large to medium-size organizations. Senior management concerns include

- Shortages of specialized talents.
- Lack of experienced/tested managers to manage new operations and who have the potential to progress to executive-level positions.
- Substantial costs associated with RIF's, relocations, recruitment of high salary levels. Personnel costs are high.
- Legal and regulatory factors that are imposing demands on current management practices. The threat of substantial costs associated with discrimination suits are ever present.
- Improvement of productivity of professional and managerial-level personnel. This is seen to be crucial if a business is to remain vigorous.
- Providing career opportunities and a working environment that will attract, motivate, and retain the talent needed.
- Changing employee attitudes toward work and careers that are causing management to review current human resource policies/practices.

The attention being given human resource planning represents a broadening of the dimensions of the personnel function and increasing involvement of line managers in personnel matters. Operating executives and mid-level managers are increasing their awareness and interest in human resource planning issues: forecasting future needs, career management, and performance management.

The consultative service industry is growing. Many organizations are reducing internal staff and hiring consultants on an "as needed" basis to reduce costs. Company personnel staffs are assuming an increasing role as contractor coordinators for management training, career development programs, performance measuring systems, relocation programs, reduction in force, benefit/compensation and labor relations services.

This approach requires the guidance of professional consultants to management, who keep abreast of the latest in behavioral science "technology" and its application to businesses. The present supply of management training, performance measurement, benefit/compensation, and labor relation services seem to be more than adequate for current demand. The consulting areas of reduction in force and career development programs seem to have an adequate supply for current needs. Consulting services for improving productivity through employee "fit" and dual career relocation considerations appear to be inadequate.

Companies and government agencies will continue to consolidate and restructure in the short run. An increased number of mid- and upper-level personnel will be let go as organizations become "lean." Companies and agencies concerned with their long-range public image and/or humanistic personnel policies will desire to use OPC when terminating upper-level management *if the dollars are available*. With large layoffs of either blue- or white-collar employees we expect to see increased use of group training in job search techniques.

As recovery of the economy takes place, we expect to see medium-large size and fast-growing companies start to use the concept of inplacement counseling to maximize managerial fits. This type of counseling will probably be limited to upper-level management positions. In an effort to retain talented personnel in these new lean organizations, we expect to see companies implement more in-house career development programs. Counseling for "trouble" employees will become part of personnel policy, but use will be limited to the "talented" ones the company wants to keep for *technical* reasons. Rapid growth industries will see a need to use inplacement counseling services to keep a talented first team together and maintain their competitive edge.

There will be continued steady use of outplacement counseling (OPC) by large companies and those concerned with their public image. OPC will be primarily made available to upper-level managers, executives, and increasingly to mid-level managers.

Relocation of personnel will receive increased attention by large companies. We see two issues emerging. First is the issue of relocating an individual where dual careers in the family are involved. Second is the increased costs of relocation and whether relocations are cost effective in terms of management development and succession selection.

We don't see preretirement counseling as a major personnel concern of companies. Preretirement programs will be largely administered internally. Developing/implementing these programs may require outside consultant assistance.

Index